EUROPEAN AND AFRICAN STEREOTYPES
IN TWENTIETH-CENTURY FICTION

EUROPEAN AND AFRICAN STEREOTYPES IN TWENTIETH-CENTURY FICTION

Sarah L. Milbury-Steen

© Sarah L. Milbury-Steen 1980

All rights reserved. No part of this publication may be reproduced or transmitted, in any form or by any means, without permission

First published 1980 by
THE MACMILLAN PRESS LTD
*London and Basingstoke
Companies and representatives
throughout the world*

Reproduced from copy supplied
printed and bound in Great Britain
by Billing and Sons Limited
Guildford, London, Oxford, Worcester

British Library Cataloguing in Publication Data

Milbury-Steen, Sarah L.
European and African stereotypes
in twentieth-century fiction
1. West Africa in literature
2. Ethnic attitudes in literature
3. African fiction (English) — Africa, West — History and criticism
4. English fiction — History and criticism
5. Africa in literature
6. African fiction (French) — History and criticism
7. French fiction — History and criticism
I. Title
823'.9' 120932   PR9340.5

ISBN 0 – 333 – 29143 – 3

In Memory of Bill

Contents

Foreword		ix
Acknowledgements		xi
	PART ONE: EUROPEANS LOOK AT AFRICANS	
1	Origins of African Stereotypes in British Colonial Novels	3
2	Origins of African Stereotypes in French Colonial Novels	20
3	Stereotypes Preserved: *A Yellow Napoleon*, *The Heart of the Matter*, *Batouala*, and *Koffi*	40
4	Stereotypes Contradicted: *The Leopard Priestess* and *Toum*	66
5	Stereotypes Transcended: *Mister Johnson* and *Va-t'en avec les tiens!*	78
	PART TWO: AFRICANS LOOK AT EUROPEANS	
6	Origins of European Stereotypes in West African Novels	97
7	Stereotypes Preserved: *Arrow of God*; *One Man, One Matchet*; *Houseboy*; and *Climbié*	124
8	Stereotypes Contradicted: *The African* and *Ambiguous Adventure*	149
9	Stereotypes Transcended: *The Land's Lord* and *The Radiance of the King*	161
Conclusion		176
Bibliography		178
Index		184

Foreword

This study of contrasting and reciprocal views of Africans and Europeans in British, French and West African novels approaches literature in terms of character and content. In it nonliterary factors have been weighed quite heavily, for cross-cultural perception is basically a historical, psychological and sociological process. The greatest potential is achieved in novels where this phenomenon is treated dynamically, showing the reader the changes which occur either internally in the minds of the characters as they adjust to individuals of another culture or externally in their modified behaviour. Unfortunately, the very complexity of this adaptive process, so difficult for most novelists to articulate, invites reduction through the use of stereotypes which often serve as simplification devices.

All of the novels examined here are twentieth-century works, published between 1921 and 1976, and all are recognisably set in West Africa, except for one French novel placed in Central Africa. Whenever feasible, novels in the same language with similar plots have been selected as a further means of synchronising the comparison. For example, the life of a house-boy in francophone Africa prior to independence is depicted by Gaston Joseph in *Koffi: roman vrai d'un noir* and Ferdinand Oyono in *Houseboy*. As for the images themselves, no effort has been made to gloss over their variety. Diversity of image has been a major criterion in choosing the novels in order to present the reader with compound images containing both positive and negative characterisations instead of a single image derived from stereotypes repeatedly found in each novel studied. The images of sixteen novels have been analysed with special emphasis placed on works which preserve, contradict and transcend stereotypes in each of the four literatures. Hopefully the reader, as a result of these measures, will be brought to a more complete understanding of the ways in which European and African characters view each other.

This book owes a great deal to the cooperation and goodwill of others whom I wish to acknowledge. Much of the research was financed by a Cross–Cultural Fellowship and was facilitated by the Indiana University Inter–Library Loan Office. I am particularly grateful to Emile Snyder, Phyllis Klotman, Breon Mitchell, Patrick O'Meara, Jean Meeh Goosebrink and William Cohen for their many helpful criticisms, and to Sue Rasmussen, Janet Gray and Margaret Beun for typing various drafts of the manuscript. Throughout this project I have received the moral support of my parents and friends, but most of all I would like to thank John for his steadfast love, and little Blythe for her happy smiles.

Brighton
March 1979

Acknowledgements

For permission to reprint material in this volume, grateful acknowledgement is made to the holders of copyright, publishers or representatives named below:

For excerpts from *A Yellow Napoleon* by Arthur E. Southon, copyright © 1928 by Hodder & Stoughton. All rights reserved. Reprinted by permission of Hodder & Stoughton Limited.

For excerpts from *Ambiguous Adventure* by C. H. Kane, trans. by Katherine Woods, copyright © 1963 by Walker & Co. Reprinted by permission of Walker & Co., Inc.

For specified excerpts from *Arrow of God* by Chinua Achebe (John Day Company). Copyright © 1964 by Chinua Achebe. Reprinted by permission of Harper & Row, Publishers, Inc. and of Bolt & Watson Ltd.

For excerpts from *Batouala: A True Black Novel* by René Maran, trans. by Barbara Beck and Alexandre Mbouko, copyright © in English translation Black Orpheus Press, Inc. 1972. Reprinted by permission of Black Orpheus Press, Inscape Corporation and of Heinemann Educational Books Ltd.

For excerpts from *Climbié* by Bernard B. Dadié, trans. by Karen C. Chapman, copyright © Editions Seghers and Bernard B. Dadié 1956 and © in English translation Heinemann Educational Books 1971. Reprinted by permission of Editions Seghers.

For excerpts from *Essai de Manuel de la langue néouolé parlée dans la partie occidentale de la Côte d'Ivoire* by Georges Thomann (Ernest Leroux, 1905). Reprinted by permission of Presses Universitaires de France.

For 'The White Man and the Negro' from *Folk-Tales of Angola: Fifty Tales, with Ki-Mbundu Text, Literal English Translation, Introduction, and Notes* by Heli Chatelain (Negro Universities Press, 1969). Reprinted by permission of Greenwood Press, Inc.

For excerpts from *Koffi: roman vrai d'un noir* by Gaston Joseph

(Editions du Monde Nouveau, 1922). Reprinted by permission of Madame Gaston Joseph.

For excerpts from Ruth Finnegan, *Limba Stories and Story-Telling*, © Oxford University Press 1967. Reprinted by permission of Oxford University Press.

For excerpts from *Houseboy* by Ferdinand Oyono, trans. by John Reed (Heinemann Educational Books, 1974). Reprinted by permission of Heinemann Educational Books Ltd. Reprinted by permission of Macmillan Publishing Co, Inc. from *Boy!* by Ferdinand Oyono. Translated from the French by John Reed. Translation: © John Reed 1966.

For brief excerpts from *Mister Johnson* by Joyce Cary (Harper & Row, 1951). Reprinted by permission of Harper & Row, Publishers, Inc. and of Curtis Brown Ltd.

For excerpts from *One Man, One Matchet* by T. M. Aluko (Heinemann Educational Books, 1962). Reprinted by permission of Heinemann Educational Books Ltd.

For the first stanza of 'The White Man's Burden' from *Rudyard Kipling's Verse, Definitive Version* (Hodder & Stoughton, 1943). Reprinted by permission of the National Trust of Great Britain through the agency of A. P. Watt Ltd.

For excerpts from *The Heart of the Matter* by Graham Greene. Copyright 1948, copyright © renewed 1971 by Graham Greene. Reprinted by permission of Viking Penguin Inc. Permission governing editions published by William Heinemann and the Bodley Head granted by Laurence Pollinger Ltd.

For excerpts from *The Land's Lord* by T. Obinkaram Echewa (Heinemann Educational Books, 1976). Reprinted by permission of Heinemann Educational Books Ltd. Permission to quote passages from *The Land's Lord* by T. Obinkaram Echewa, © 1976 by T. Obinkaram Echewa was granted for the territory of the U.S.A. by the author's agent Max Gartenberg.

For excerpts from *The Leopard Priestess* by Robert S. Rattray (T. Butterworth, 1934). Reprinted by permission of Mrs Noelle Rattray. Reprinted by permission of Hawthorn Books, Inc. from *The Leopard Priestess* by Robert S. Rattray, copyright © 1935 by Appleton–Century Croft. All rights reserved.

For excerpts from *The Radiance of the King* by Camara Laye, trans. by James Kirkup (Collins, 1965). Reprinted by permission of Collins Publishers. Reprinted with permission of Macmillan Publishing Co., Inc. from *The Radiance of the King* by Camara Laye.

Acknowledgements

Translated from the French by James Kirkup. Copyright © 1971 by Macmillan Publishing Co, Inc.

For excerpts from *Toum* by Louis Faivre, pseud. of Robert Louis Delavignette (Bernard Grasset, 1926) and for excerpts from *Va-t'en avec les tiens!* by Christine Garnier (Bernard Grasset, 1951). Reprinted by permission of Editions Bernard Grasset.

PART ONE: EUROPEANS LOOK AT AFRICANS

1 Origins of African Stereotypes in British Colonial Novels

The writings of European racial and colonial theorists, ethnocentric anthropologists, and popular adventurers in the late nineteenth and early twentieth centuries permit one to discover which stereotypes came together to form both the British and French literary images of Africans. England will be dealt with first, since the writings of Robert Knox—a Scottish anatomist devoted almost exclusively to the race question—were known by Arthur de Gobineau, who will serve as the starting point for a discussion of French pseudo-scientific racism in the next chapter. In the estimation of Philip Curtin, the basic premises of Knox were incorporated recognisably into the theories of Gobineau, for there was a fair amount of awareness and exchange between the racist theoreticians of both countries.[1]

During the period cited above, racist theorists in Europe and America applied the methods of empirical observation and logical deduction to their work to prove their points 'scientifically'. The fact that their basic premises were later discounted as fallacious did not necessarily decrease the circulation of their conclusions among the general populace, even comparatively recently. The central belief of pseudo–scientific racists has been identified by Curtin as:

> ... the proposition that race was one of the principal determinants of attitudes, endowments, capabilities, and inherent tendencies among human beings. Race thus seemed to determine the course of human history.[2]

Throughout the first part of the nineteenth century in both England and France, there was a great deal of controversy between the advocates of monogenesis (called unitarianism in France) and those of polygenesis concerning the origin of man.³ The former, strongly rooted in the eighteenth century concept of the 'Great Chain of Being', insisted that even though the African ranked below the European both physically and socially he was still of the same species and capable of improvement over time. Their orientation was highly Christian and Biblical, designating Adam and Eve as the common ancestors of all men. Against them stood the polygenists who maintained that each race had been created separately and that the consequent differences between races were permanent. David Hume used the polygenist argument in the eighteenth century to declare the superiority of European culture and the causal relationship between race and culture:

> There never was a civilised nation of any other complexion than white, nor even any individual eminent either in action or speculation. No ingenious manufactures amongst them, no arts, no sciences . . . Such a uniform and constant difference could not happen, in so many countries and ages, if nature had not made an original distinction betwixt these breeds of men.⁴

As the nineteenth century progressed, the polygenist cause gathered more proponents than the monogenist until the discoveries of Charles Darwin reduced both schools of thought to irrelevancy. For the monogenists this defeat was particularly painful, since it not only collapsed whatever scientific basis they had previously used but also elevated scientific truth over Christian orthodoxy. On the other hand, the racist polygenist merely needed to discard his idea of multiple creations, change his terminology, and employ the idea of natural selection to demonstrate that races differed considerably from each other.

Even before the advent of Darwinism, Robert Knox had made suspect a primary belief of monogenists—i.e. that all races can interbreed and produce fertile progeny.⁵ He postulated that first generation mulattoes might possibly be as fertile as their parents, but succeeding ones would show the predominance of one of the 'pure' ancestral races, because he thought hybrid races were not as hardy as uncrossed ones. Since one of the outstanding characteristics of most of the racist theorists in England and on the Continent was their eclecticism, it is not at all extraordinary that Knox on this point was reviving the false data developed about a hundred years earlier by Long, nor that Broca in France would later appropriate it as part of his proof of polygenesis. Nonetheless, Knox was not truly a polygenist, for he posited an evolution in which all species were represented potentially at the time of the original creation, then later developed according to a plan which began with 'animals lowest on the scale, acquatic chiefly; then the mollusca and shellfish; then fishes; next birds, the quadrupeds, and, lastly man'.[6] Later Darwin would fill the gap in Knox's concept by supplying the idea of exactly how this evolutionary process occurred.

In terms of racial hierarchies, Knox had no doubt that the dark races were inferior, even though he considered the Negro superior to all other persons of colour.[7] He based his assumptions partially upon the fact that the Negro was capable of living in areas in Africa that had proven fatal to the white man. He credited the Negro with the possibility of reaching a certain degree of civilisation, of occasionally exhibiting great energy, of showing some level of intelligence in commercial matters on the coast of Africa, and of having some sensibilities to music. However, he still stressed that all dark races suffered from mental deficiencies, especially in the areas of pure reason, curiosity and observation. He also formulated a theory of stasis, claiming that Negro civilisation had reached its apex in the distant past, then stagnated:

> In central Africa the true black or negro race seems to have attained his ultimatum centuries ago. He has his own form of civilisation, but unfortunately it includes neither literature, art, nor science.[8]

The concept of the frozen state of African civilisation later enjoyed wide acceptance at home and abroad. For the builders of colonial empires it provided a seemingly irrefutable rationale, since only Europeans could bring progress to sluggish African societies.

The ideas of Knox that eventually found their way into colonialistic propaganda were decidedly taken out of context, for Knox himself was opposed to colonialism. To him the presumption of imposing the culture of one group of people on another was foolhardy, for 'each race must act for itself, and work out its own destiny; display its own tendencies; be the maker of its own fortunes, be they good or evil'.[9]

Charles Darwin technically never applied his discovery of biological evolution to social situations. Yet there is a significant violation of his principle of detachment in a passage in *The Descent of Man* in which he describes his disgust upon seeing a group of Fuegian 'barbarians':

> But there can hardly be a doubt that we are descended from barbarians. The astonishment which I felt on first seeing a party of Fuegians on a wild and broken shore will never be forgotten by me, for the reflection at once rushed into my mind—such were our ancestors. These men were absolutely naked and bedaubed with paint, their long hair was tangled, their mouths frothed with excitement, and their expression was wild, startled and distrustful. They possessed hardly any arts, and like wild animals lived on what they could catch; they had no government, and were merciless to everyone not of their own small tribe. He who has seen a savage in his native land will not feel much shame, if forced to acknowledge that the blood of some more humble creature flows in his veins. For my own part I would as soon be descended from that heroic little monkey, who braved his dread enemy in order to save the life of his keeper, or from that old baboon, who descending from the mountains, carried away in triumph his young comrade from a crowd of astonished dogs—as from a savage who delights to torture his enemies, offers up bloody sacrifices, practises infanticide without remorse, treats his wives like slaves, knows no decency, and is haunted by the grossest superstitions.[10]

By the time Darwin wrote this account in the 1870s, the image of the African as savage and primitive had long been a stock European opinion. This identification had its literary roots in the eighteenth century when 'the noble savage' and 'the bestial savage' became conventions of abolitionist and pro–slavery literature respectively. Despite the fact that Darwin's paragraph does not specifically mention Africans, it is reasonable to conjecture that readers in the late nineteenth century had little difficulty in projecting his description of Fuegians onto Africans. Note the manner in which he animalises the savage and anthropomorphises the monkey, endowing the human being with the traits of 'the bestial savage'—cruelty, brutality, and pitilessness—and the monkey with those of 'the noble savage'—loyalty, bravery, and heroism.

The development of social Darwinism was the work of Herbert Spencer who thereby earned from Darwin the epithet 'the great expounder of the principle of evolution'.[11] In developing the philosophy of social Darwinism, Spencer showed a great deal of interest in primitive man as an aid to understanding the cultural and social evolution of modern man. Since it was a widely held assumption that non-Western civilisations were really living museums of earlier levels of human progress, ethnocentric anthropologists relied upon studies of African tribes as the basis for theories about the mind and activities of prehistoric Western man. Drawing from field accounts of travellers and ethnologists, Spencer characterised primitive man as blessed with superior powers of sensory perception and careful observation, but cursed with deficient powers of abstraction, inquiry, intellectual curiosity and constructive imagination.[12] He made the analogy between African tribesmen and children by insisting that, 'the intellectual traits of the uncivilised . . . are traits recurring in the children of the civilised,' offering as proof:

> Infancy shows us an absorption in sensations and perceptions akin to that which characterised the savage.
> Children are ever dramatising the lives of adults; and savages, along with their other mimicries, similarly dramatise the actions of their civilised visitors. Want of power to discriminate between useless and useful facts, characterises the juvenile mind, as it does the mind of primitive man.[13]

Since the primitive was less evolved than civilised man, he was equally deficient, in Spencer's estimation, on the emotional level.[14] For example, he ascribed to the 'savage' an inability to display higher emotions or to resist acting upon every desire and impulse. He endorsed the saying, 'the savage has the mind of a child with the passions of a man', as a fairly accurate depiction of the relationship between the mental and emotional sides of primitive man. Note that he carefully did not credit him with the emotions, but only the passions, of a man, for that would have substantially weakened his claim that the primitive differed from the civilised man in his childish impulse, mirth and improvidence.

Spencer's descriptions of primitive man were echoed in the twentieth century in the works of anthropologists and devotees of the race question in both England and the United States. Under the aegis of science, the drive to make these qualitative differences demonstrable on a quantitative scale continued, so that even as late as 1904 Edward Tylor advocated Samuel George Morton's pre-1839 method of filling the cranial cavity of skulls with seeds to prove objectively the intellectual inferiority of the savage.[15] Three years later, Jerome Dowd in *The Negro Race* showed that Darwin himself had sanctioned the measuring of skulls as a method of proving evolution and distinguishing between savage and civilised races.[16] Dowd also proffered the theory that the Negro brain developed earlier than that of the white up to the age of puberty, 'in accordance with the general law that the simpler the organism the more rapidly it reaches its maximum of growth'.[17] As evidence, he cited the trend of Negro children to surpass their white classmates on the elementary school level in the coastal and forest zones of West Africa until pubescence, when:

> ... the Negro, accustomed from time immemorial to give complete reign to his sexual passions finds it difficult to keep up interest in lines of study which require the inhibitions of other interests.[18]

The rest of Dowd's analysis closely resembled Spencer's, except for his correlation of laziness with brain size and his acceptance of the standard stereotypes of Negroes as superstitious, cruel, dishonest, vain and cowardly.[19]

Even though the intelligentsia in England were fairly steeped in these concepts regarding primitive man, Franz Boas was attempting to free anthropology from the fallacy that the brain of the 'savage' was physically and mentally unlike that of civilised man. In 1909 Boas addressed himself to this problem by stating:

> It would seem that, in different races, the organisation of the mind is on the whole alike, and that the varieties of mind found in different races do not exceed, perhaps not even reach, the amount of normal individual variation in each race.[20]

He further challenged racist eugenicists by declaring that all that really separated the minds of the uncivilised from the civilised were differences of environment and personal experience.[21]

Most of the nineteenth century racist theorists and ethnologists worked purely from their armchairs, apparently accepting as valid any incident reported in the field accounts of Europeans in Africa. Such presumption was only matched by that of some of the missionaries and adventurers themselves who, in seeing an event but understanding little if anything of its cultural context, still felt qualified to interpret and generalise from it. Consequently, such writers as David Livingstone, Henry M. Stanley and Mary Kingsley both excited the British popular imagination and reinforced biased opinions of Africans and Africa. Their books served as practical applications of ideas already current in England, for according to Curtin, the British image of Africa was set by the 1850s in both the popular and educated press:

> Its [the image's] major affirmations were the 'common knowledge' of the educated classes. Thereafter, when new generations of explorers or administrators went to Africa, they went with a prior impression of what they would find. Most often, they found it, and their writings in turn confirmed the older image—or at most altered it only slightly.[22]

David Livingstone and his brother Charles shared with their British contemporaries the opinion that African societies had advanced to a certain degree and then stagnated, remaining 'in the same rude state for a great number of centuries'.[23] They also subscribed to the idea that racial inter-breeding was unnatural and negative, for in describing the treatment Portuguese half-castes gave their slaves, they endorsed a proverb once told them by a Portuguese acquaintance, 'God made white men and God made black men, but the devil made half-castes'.[24] They revived an earlier abolitionist argument that it was the institution of slavery which debased Africans, claiming that those who had never been enslaved would be ranked by an impartial witness as 'very much higher in the scale of intelligence, industry and manhood' than those who had been slaves.[25] In relating anecdotes involving African encounters with Western technology, the implication was generally given that Africans were childlike, seeing the simplest invention as a proof of the 'white man's magic'.[26] However, in all fairness to the Livingstones, it must be emphasised that they showed more sympathy towards the customs and people they met than most explorers, who usually discussed tribes purely in terms of how useful they had been to them.

The works of Henry M. Stanley, written in a more energetic style, showed both a departure from and a respect for Dr Livingstone's more tolerant approach towards Africans. He summarised the missionary's attitude in this way, affirming the 'white man's burden':

> He [Livingstone] can be charmed with the primitive simplicity of Ethiop's dusky children, with whom he has spent so many years of his life; he has a sturdy faith in their capabilities; sees virtues in them where others see nothing but savagery; and whenever he has gone among them, he has sought to elevate a people that were apparently forgotten of God and Christian man.[27]

Although Stanley claimed that he was willing to accept Africans as his brothers, the phraseology of his mental question, 'have these men—these black savages from pagan Africa—the qualities which make man lovable among his fellows?' preserves some African stereotypes.[28]

His opinion of half-castes was strongly condemnatory, branding them as 'cringing and hypocritical, cowardly and debased, treacherous and mean', and singling out the Zanzibar half-caste as the 'syphilitic, blear-eyed, pallid-skinned, abortion of an African Arab'.[29] He characterised Africans as childlike, idle, musical, imitative, ignorant, superstitious, cannibalistic, cruel and improvident.[30] In describing physical appearance, he generally found Africans ugly, except when their features were more Caucasian than Negroid, in which case character evaluation soared considerably as well. The people most disgusting to the explorer were the Pygmies, one of whom he regarded as a candidate for Darwin's 'missing link':

> The monkey-eyed woman had a remarkable pair of mischievous orbs, protruding lips overhanging her chin, a prominent abdomen, narrow, flat chest, sloping shoulders, long arms, feet turned greatly inwards and very short lower legs, as being fitly characteristic of the link sought between the average modern humanity and its Darwinian progenitors, and certainly deserving of being classed as an extremely low, degraded, almost bestial type of a human being.[31]

Even though Stanley focused upon a particular individual in the passage above, he often resorted to the fallacy of extrapolating about the nature of Africans from the evidence of one or two tribesmen. However, it worked both ways in his case, for he tended to think of himself collectively as well, proudly perceiving each of his accomplishments in Africa as a forward advance in establishing among Africans 'the honour and reputation of white men'.³²

Over twenty years later in 1897, Mary Kingsley concurred with Stanley's suggestion of an African as the Darwinian link by placing the lower specimens of both the Negro and Bantu races on the 'border-line that separates man from the anthropoid apes'.³³ Yet most of her criticism was reserved for the partially westernised African, whom she detested as a travesty of civilised man. At best, she claimed, the missionary education he had received was only a veneer, sufficient enough for him to imitate the white man ludicrously and treat his uneducated brothers contemptuously.³⁴ An enthusiastic advocate of Western technology—even praising a railway engine as a 'manifestation of the superiority of my race—' she accused Africans of mechanical ineptitude, insisting that:

> ... unless under white direction, the African has never made an even fourteenth–rate piece of cloth or pottery, or a machine tool, picture, sculpture, and that he had never even risen to the level of picture writing.³⁵

As a result of this deficiency, she concluded that the African mind looked at all things 'spiritually', while the Western mind examined them 'materialistically'—the essential way for progress and technology.³⁶ Moreover, as an imperialist and white supremacist, she held two principles as inviolable: (1) the African could only achieve modernisation through colonialism and (2) he would never truly be equal with whites, since she doubted whether Europeans could 'ever drag the black up to their own particular summit in the mountain range of civilisation'.³⁷

Shortly before her death, her opinions seemed to mellow, for in a letter to the Liberian editor of *The New Africa*,³⁸ Mary Kingsley pleaded for mutual understanding between the two races, regretting that:

> The stay–at–home statesmen think that Africans are all awful savages or silly children—people who can only be dealt with on a reformatory penitentiary line. This view you know is not mine, nor that of the very small party—the scientific ethnologists—who deal with Africa; but it is the view of the statesmen and the general public and the mission public, in African affairs.³⁹

She hoped that the editor and other Africans, capable of grasping the fundamentals of English culture, would help Britishers comprehend African institutions. Her real motive, however, was one of enlightened colonialism rather than altruism, for she was eager for colonial statesmen, once they became aware of African values, to permit Africans to develop along their 'own lines', according to their own racial destiny. Her primary fear as a racial determinist was that colonial policy, failing to observe that races evolve very differently from each other, would destroy aspects of African culture that should be preserved.

The correlation of the ideas of Livingstone, Stanley and Kingsley with those of the theorists examined earlier has demonstrated a fairly frozen image of Africans toward the end of the nineteenth century. A further case for its pervasiveness may be made by turning to British colonial policy and practice in order to evaluate the degree to which these theories were applied by colonials on the field.

While the British advocates of imperialism at first thought primarily in terms of white settlement colonies, the 'scramble' for Africa in the 1880s forced their conception of colonialism to expand. It came to include not only large black colonies in tropical Africa, but also the ideas of commercial and cultural imperialism championed by Joseph Chamberlain and Rudyard Kipling. Chamberlain, a successful Birmingham manufacturer who was appointed head of the Colonial Office in 1895, claimed that the 'British Empire is commerce'.[40] Kipling gave expression to Britain's 'civilising mission' in his poem 'The White Man's Burden' which appeared in the London *Times* on 4 February 1899.[41]

From the time of the European partition of Africa until the First World War, Britain followed an empirical system of 'indirect rule' instead of her earlier colonial policy of 'identity', or assimilation.[42] Although identity had worked fairly well with small populations, it was doubtful whether it could accommodate Britain's rapid acquisition of territories and subjects. Furthermore, identity had not always proved successful, particularly in South Africa, and had earned some opposition at home.[43] Indirect rule consequently became Britain's 'on the spot' solution to the problem of managing large numbers of 'natives' with a minimum of English personnel and expenditure. Since it utilised traditional rulers who had pledged allegiance to the Crown, it permitted the district administrator to devote his time first to intertribal pacification and suppression of the slave trade, then to the creation of courts and the collection of taxes.

The man who transformed 'indirect rule' from a makeshift manoeuvre into a progressive and workable theory of Native Authority was Lord Lugard. Seeking not merely to preserve local traditional power but to revitalise it and direct it toward political and economic advancement, Lugard described his system as:

> two sets of Rulers—the British and the Native—working either separately or in cooperation, but a single Government in which the Native Chiefs have clearly defined duties and an acknowledged *status*, equally with the British officials.[44]

Accordingly, the local rulers were granted 'the ultimate title to all land, the right to appoint Emirs and all the officers of state, the right of legislation and of taxation'.[45] Lugard first applied his system of Indirect Rule in Northern Nigeria while he was its High Commissioner (1900–6) and later throughout the rest of the country during his years as Governor of the North and South, then Governor General of Nigeria (1912–19). His book, *The Dual Mandate in British Tropical Africa* (1922), offered a full explanation of his programme of Native Authority and served as the blueprint for British colonial policy between the First and Second World Wars.

This highly influential work presents an image of Africans not so very different from that painted by earlier writers. Even though Lugard spares us the excesses of some of his fellow colonial administrators such as Sir Harry Hamilton Johnston, he nonetheless characterises Africans as one 'of the child races of the world' and 'a race which illustrates every stage in the evolution of human society'.[46]

In describing individuals of Bantu stock in Nigeria, Lugard invokes a number of familiar stereotypes:

> In character and temperament the typical African of this race-type is a happy, thriftless, excitable person, lacking in self-control, discipline, and foresight, naturally courageous, and naturally courteous and polite, full of personal vanity, with little sense of veracity, fond of music, and 'loving weapons as an oriental loves jewellery'. His thoughts are concentrated on the events and feelings of the moment, and he suffers little from apprehension for the future, or grief for the past.[47]

Despite his contention, 'there is no colour bar in British Africa, and the educated native enjoys the fullest liberty,' *de facto* social segregation did exist and educated nationalist leaders often suffered curtailment of their civil rights.[48] Oliver and Fage claim that the colour bar was established before the First World War as soon as health conditions and tropical medicine were advanced enough to allow British wives to accompany their husbands.[49] In order to provide for social recreation, growing enclaves of Britishers instituted 'the Club' which brought even greater cohesion to the whites, and distance from the blacks. Hannah Arendt has designated aloofness, both political and social, as a distinctive feature of British colonial officials, who believed that their higher plane of civilisation rightfully isolated them from Africans.[50]

Even though Lugard's system was applied throughout Britain's African colonies, it eventually proved to be far from ideal. According to Joyce Cary in *The Case for African Freedom* (1941), indirect rule often encouraged the preservation of traditional institutions that were no longer responsive to the needs of the people.[51] He suggested that this policy 'intended to secure native liberty; not to enlarge native freedom, or to raise standards of living' should be replaced by a new one of full scale economic and social development that would 'prepare the African to take his part as the full citizen of a *modern* state, in a *modern* world'.[52]

The Colonial Development Act of 1945 marked a British commitment not only to the old goal of readying dependent peoples for self-government, but also to the new one of improving their standard of living. The implementation of development projects in the colonies necessitated the recruitment of large numbers of technically and professionally trained Europeans. In order to attract qualified personnel, the Government offered them inflated salaries, sizable travel allowances, and comfortable housing during their stay in Africa. As technical assistants, they lived in special expatriate communities and generally mixed with Africans only at work.

This type of segregation added to white self-sufficiency and clannishness, contributing to an intensified antagonism between Europeans and Africans. A deep source of frustration was the disparity between European and African wages, traditionally justified by the 'fact' that African workers were lazy and inefficient. The drive for self-government, headed mainly by young educated Africans, gained momentum from the irritation of the increased British presence in the colonies after the Second World War. By

1961 nationalistic movements had succeeded in winning independence in practically all of Britain's African colonies.

Kenneth Little, drawing on the research of Leonard Barnes, has demonstrated that service in the colonies was one way of moving from the middle to the upper class in British society.[53] The colonial class at home had sufficient prominence and prestige, in the main, to convince the general public that their opinions, founded on first-hand knowledge through colonial experience, were correct. Often when their claims were unmasked as prejudices, popular belief was still not suspended, causing Little to cite the personal impressions made by colonials as an important factor in shaping modern British attitudes towards Negroes.

Another significant avenue for the personal perspectives of colonial officers and missionaries lay in literature itself, for many of them at some point in their careers tried their hand at writing a novel. Their novels may be broadly characterised as either (1) an adventure story, often with romantic intrigue, which has no true involvement with the native—derived from Kipling's early stories and the works of Haggard—or (2) a psychological one, dealing with cultural conflict, race relations, colonial realities or self-identification in the manner of Conrad.[54] The novels read for this study which belonged to the first category tended to utilise Africans as shadow figures in an imperialistic drama of heroism in which natives were to be conquered and civilised. Accordingly, the African characters who played more than the role of knick-knacks were either loyal servants, cunning villains, Westernised Africans or uncivilised primitives.

The attitudes towards 'good' servants included a certain affection, albeit the kind given a house pet, for even though the servant accompanied the master on lonely bush treks, he did not serve as a personal confidant. As for villains, by far the most treacherous was the mulatto who had inherited the worst traits of both races, devoting his superior European intelligence to the deception of ignorant black tribesmen. Those Africans who imitated or 'aped' Western ways were especially ridiculed because of their impudence in presuming that they could attain the level of British civilisation.[55] Even Lord Lugard had little patience with Europeanised Africans whom he alleged differed not only mentally but also physically from regular natives as a consequence of their in-breeding with only Westernised Africans and their adoption of European clothes, inappropriate for the tropics.[56] The uncivilised primitive, while always greatly inferior to the British, was not always hostile and savage, even though native cruelty, human sacrifice and cannibalism were frequently presented as justifications for British imperialism. The childlike African was just as popular in colonial literature, since his ignorance and need for guidance appealed less sensationally to the British sense of moral responsibility for the enlightenment of the 'benighted'.

In the second group of novels—those with a psychological orientation—authors gazed either outwardly or inwardly in order to arrive at a universal experience. Joyce Cary favoured the first approach, since it permitted him to present the clash of cultures in Nigeria as a microcosm of the obsessions basic to all men. Graham Greene, on the other hand, quested for identity in Africa, searching for a primal part of his subconscious self. For him and other Freudian authors, Africa was a labyrinth with the African at its centre, representing the racial childhood which the European must claim and accept.[57]

Hammond and Jablow charge that British colonial novels of this century have merely preserved and formalised nineteenth century views of Africans.[58] The fact that this phenomenon of transfer occurs in French literature as well reveals that British and French images of Africans were largely shaped in the same mould of European superiority.

NOTES

1. Philip D. Curtin, *The Image of Africa: British Ideas and Action, 1780–1850* (Madison: University of Wisconsin Press, 1964) p. 381.
2. Ibid., p. 29.
3. For a good account of this controversy, see Curtin, pp. 40–1 and 364–9, and William B. Cohen, 'Literature and Race: Nineteenth Century Fiction, Blacks, and Africa 1800–1880', *Race and Class*, vol. xvi, No. 2 (Oct. 1974) pp. 184–5.
4. Curtin, p. 41.
5. Ibid., pp. 368–9.
6. Ibid., p. 369.
7. Robert Knox, *The Races of Men: A Fragment* (Philadelphia: Lea and Blanchard, 1850; reprinted, Miami: Mnemosye Pub. Co., 1969) pp. 190–1, 163.
8. Ibid., p. 303.
9. Ibid., pp. 304, 210.
10. Charles Darwin, *The Descent of Man and Selection in Relation to Sex*, revised ed. (New York: Merrill & Baker, 1874) p. 613.
11. Herbert Spencer, *The Evolution of Society: Selections from Herbert Spencer's*

Principles of Sociology, ed. Robert L. Carneiro (Chicago: Univ. of Chicago Press, 1967) p. lvi.
12. Herbert Spencer, 'The Primitive Man—Intellectual,' in *Source Book for Social Origins*, ed. William I. Thomas (Chicago: Univ. of Chicago Press, 1909) pp. 201–10.
13. Ibid., pp. 211–2.
14. Herbert Spencer, 'The Primitive Man—Emotional,' Op. cit. pp. 186, 190–1.
15. Edward B. Tylor, *Anthropology: An Introduction to the Study of Man and Civilisation* (New York: D. Appleton & Co. 1904) p. 60, and Curtin, p. 367.
16. Jerome Dowd, *The Negro Races: A Sociological Study* (Chicago: Afro–Am Press, 1969) p. 356. This book was originally published in 1907.
17. Ibid., p. 360.
18. Ibid., p. 360.
19. Ibid., pp. 366, 371, 376, 388, 394–5.
20. Franz Boas, 'The Mind of Primitive Man,' in *Source Book for Social Origins*, ed. William I. Thomas (Chicago: Univ. of Chicago Press, 1909) p. 155. This concept was incorporated into Boas' book *The Mind of Primitive Man* which was published in 1911 and revised by the author in 1938. Considered a dangerous work by white supremacists at home and abroad, its German translation, *Kultur und Rasse*, was one of the books burned by the Nazis on 10 May 1933. In the preface to the 1938 edition Boas remarks:

> There is no fundamental difference in the ways of thinking of primitive and civilised man. A close connection between race and personality has never been established. The concept of racial type as commonly used even in scientific literature is misleading and requires a logical as well as a biological redefinition. *The Mind of Primitive Man* (New York: Free Press, 1963), p. 17.

21. Ibid., p. 155.
22. Curtin, p. vi.
23. David Livingstone and Charles Livingstone, *Narrative of an Expedition to the Zambesi and its Tributaries; and of the Discovery of the Lakes Shirwa and Nyassa 1858–1864* (New York: Harper & Bros., 1866) p. 627.
24. Ibid., p. 56.
25. Ibid., p. 525.
26. Ibid., pp. 583–4.
27. Henry M. Stanley, *How I Found Livingstone. Travels, Adventures and Discoveries in Central Africa* (New York: Arno & The New York Times, 1970. Reprint of New York: Scribner, Armstrong & Co., 1872) p. 438.
28. Ibid., pp. 9–10.
29. Ibid., p. 8.
30. Ibid., pp. 25, 359, 549. Henry M. Stanley, *In Darkest Africa or the Quest, Rescue and Retreat of Emin Governor of Equatoria*, vols. i and ii (New York: Charles Scribner's Sons, 1890), vol. i, pp. 155, 182; vol. ii, p. 29. Richard Stanley and Alan Neame, eds., *The Exploration Diaries of H. M. Stanley* (New York: The Vanguard Press, Inc., 1961) pp. 73, 82, 45.
31. Stanley, *In Darkest Africa* . . . , vol. i, pp. 374–5.
32. Stanley and Neame, p. 72.

33. Mary H. Kingsley, *Travels in West Africa: Congo Français, Corisco and Cameroons* (London: Frank Cass & Co. Ltd., 1965; first published by Macmillan & Co. Ltd., 1897) p. 458.
34. Ibid., pp. 660–1.
35. Mary H. Kingsley, *West African Studies* (London: Macmillan & Co. Ltd., 1901; first published in 1899) pp. 330, 670.
36. Ibid., p. 330.
37. Ibid., p. 680.
38. Ibid., pp. xvii–xviii.
39. Ibid., p. xvii.
40. Louis L. Snyder, ed., *The Imperialism Reader: Documents and Readings on Modern Expansion* (Princeton: D. Van Nostrand Co., Inc., 1962) p. 125.
41. The first stanza conveys the tone and mood of the rest of the poem:

    Take up the White Man's Burden—
    Send forth the best ye breed—
    Go bind your sons to exile
    To serve your captives' need;
    To wait in heavy harness,
    On fluttered folk and wild—
    You new caught, sullen peoples,
    Half–devil and half–child.

    From *Rudyard Kipling's Verse*, Definitive Edition (London: Hodder & Stoughton, 1943) p. 323.
42. Based on the premise that men are generally the same 'identity' was practised by Britain in the small coastal areas annexed before the 1880s. It entailed the conferral of British citizenship, the establishment of English law, and the development of legislative and municipal councils. See Margery Freda Perham's *The Colonial Reckoning: The End of Imperial Rule in Africa in the Light of British Experience* (New York: Alfred A. Knopf, 1962) p. 65.
43. A representative anti–assimilationist stand can be found in J. Scott Keltie's *The Partition of Africa* (London: Edward Stanford, 1895) p. 514:

    It is not necessary, however, indeed it would only be disastrous, to attempt to force the native into the European mould. That may come in the long run; but wherever the forcing process has been tried, especially by injudicious missionaries, the product has not been lovely.

44. Margery Perham, *Lugard*, vol. ii, *The Years of Authority, 1898–1945* (London: Collins, 1961) p. 144.
45. Ibid., p. 148.
46. Lord Lugard, *The Dual Mandate in British Tropical Africa* (Hamden, Conn.: Archon Books, 1965) p. 72.

    Sir Harry Johnston, who wrote over thirty-two works on Africa, including several novels based upon his experiences as an administrator, depicted Africans in *A History of the Colonisation of Africa by Alien Races* (Cambridge: Cambridge Univ. Press, 1905) pp. 91–2, as completely servile:

> ... the negro in general is a born slave. He is possessed of great physical strength, docility, cheerfulness of disposition, a short memory for sorrows and cruelties, and an easily aroused gratitude for kindness and just dealing. He does not suffer from home-sickness to the overbearing extent that afflicts other people torn from their homes, and, provided he is well fed, he is easily made happy ... He has little or no race-fellowship—that is to say, he has no sympathy for other negroes...

47. Ibid., p. 69.
48. Ibid., p. 86, and Thomas Hodgkin, *Nationalism in Colonial Africa* (New York: New York Univ. Press, 1963) p. 47.
49. Roland Oliver and John D. Fage, *A Short History of Africa* (Baltimore: Penguin Books, 1964) p. 206.
50. Hannah Arendt, *The Origins of Totalitarianism* (New York: Meridian Books, Inc., 1959) p. 212.
51. Joyce Cary, *The Case for African Freedom and Other Writings on Africa* (Austin: Univ. of Texas Press, 1962) p. 58.
52. Ibid., pp. 58, 60.
53. Kenneth Lindsay Little, *Negroes in Britain: A Study of Racial Relations in English Society* (London: Routledge & Kegan Paul, 1972) pp. 238–9.
54. Dorothy Hammond and Alta Jablow, *The Africa That Never Was: Four Centuries of British Writing about Africa* (New York: Twayne Publishers, Inc., 1970) p. 118. Jeffrey Meyers, *Fiction & the Colonial Experience* (Ipswich, England: The Boydell Press, 1972) pp. vii–viii.
55. Hammond and Jablow, p. 98. D. Killam, 'Fictional Sources for African Studies', *Journal of the Historical Society of Nigeria*, vol. iii, no. 2 (Dec. 1965) p. 395.
56. Lugard, pp. 79–80.
57. Hammond and Jablow, pp. 145–6; Meyers, p. viii.
58. Hammond and Jablow, pp. 122–3.

2 Origins of African Stereotypes in French Colonial Novels

The literary image of Africans prevalent in French colonial novels owes a considerable debt to the writings of pseudo–scientific racists that were published during the late nineteenth and early twentieth centuries. One important exception, however, is Count Arthur de Gobineau's celebrated work *Essai sur l'inégalité des races humaines*, which appeared between 1853 and 1855. This long treatise which most scholars, including Arendt, regard as the seminal point for the racism employed by imperialism and totalitarianism, has been clearly demonstrated by both Curtin and Cohen to be a compilation, synthetic rather than original, of earlier racist theories.[1] In this work Gobineau returned to the long–standing debate of monogenesis *vs* polygenesis, as well as the identification of language as a racial attribute; then borrowed from Knox the concept of racial purity as a requisite of racial strength; from Morton the association of physical characteristics with racial differences and mental deficiencies; and from Carus the equation of culture with race as a means of classifying mankind.[2] Even his fundamental premises that race dominated history and that civilisations declined through the degeneration of racial mixing found antecedents in Knox's assertion, 'race is everything; literature, science, art—in a word, civilisation depends on it'.[3] Gobineau's real talent was as an organiser and not a thinker, for his ability to assemble all of these ideas cohesively was without precedent.

Using the criteria of physical, mental and social characteristics, mixture or purity of blood, and moral virtues or decadence, Gobineau ranked races in a hierarchy with the white at the top, followed by the yellow, and finally the black.[4] His refutation of the theory of monogenesis was simply that the physical differences between whites and blacks were irreconcilable, since in looking at a

Negro, 'the mind involuntarily recalls the structure of a monkey'.[5] He solidified the traits variously ascribed to Africans in the past into a compact series of black stereotypes: mental deficiency, will based on instinct, abnormally acute senses of taste and smell, uncontrollable appetite, excessive sensuality, emotional instability, moral inferiority, physical cruelty, extreme laziness and a lack of both courage and pity.[6] Gobineau opposed miscegenation, for while it upgraded the lower races it enervated the higher ones.[7] Nonetheless, he claimed that artistic genius—a quality alien to all of the three 'pure' races—had arisen only after the intermixing of black and white stock.[8]

An example of the more typical appraisal of blacks as artistic nullities can be found in the work of Alfred Fouillée, an early champion of assimilation, who in 1894 concluded on the basis of field data from travellers and ethnologists that:

> The Negro race, since its advent, has not raised a single monument of art or literature; the state of its knowledge has remained rudimentary. The same thing may be said of the Negro who has come under the influence of the most cultured minds and has received a liberal education, for he has not yet executed a work of genius in any realm of intellectual activity.[9]

In addition to the faults Gobineau had attributed to the black, Fouillée accused him of being heedless of the future, overly fond of singing and dancing, afraid of solitude, and imitative like a child or monkey as a result of mental inferiority and inertia.[10] However, he did have some good qualities, conveniently, ones that made him useful to Europeans as a servant or a soldier, since he was 'appreciative of good treatment, capable of great devotion, but also capable of hating and of revenging himself cruelly'.[11] Fouillée believed that inferior races could be modified through education rather than miscegenation, since the former would bring about a lasting psychological change but the latter would only lead to racial mediocrity.[12]

One of Fouillée's leading opponents was his contemporary Gustave LeBon who contended that, 'the psychological characteristics of peoples . . . possess, like the anatomical characteristics, a high degree of fixity. It is on account of this fixity that the soul of races changes so slowly during the course of ages'.[13] He separated the races into the primitive, inferior, average and superior ones.

'Primitive races' were those that demonstrated 'no trace of culture', while the 'inferior ones', represented by the Negroes, were 'capable of attaining to the rudiments only'.[14] In discussing the 'inferior races', LeBon emphasised their mental inadequacies, especially the inability to reason or think critically, and its corollary—excessive credulity.[15] These failings plus short attention spans, poor powers of observation, and a propensity for imitation, improvidence and impulsiveness all condemned blacks to a permanent state of inferiority.[16]

LeBon, long opposed to the idea of assimilation supported by Fouillée and others, had unsuccessfully attempted to show its folly at the 1889 Colonial Congress. He regarded the theory that education could modify race as particulary ludicrous:

> A Negro or a Japanese may easily take a university degree or become a lawyer; the sort of varnish he thus acquires is however quite superficial, and has no influence on his mental constitution. What no education can give him, because they are created by heredity alone are the forms of thought, the logic, and above all the character of Western man. Our Negro or our Japanese may accumulate all possible certificates without ever attaining to the level of the average European.[17]

Comparing an educated Negro to an average European represented a certain advancement, since Gobineau had alleged that even the most inferior members of the dominant races outclassed all individuals of the lesser races in energy, activity, and intelligence.[18]

Charles Letourneau, who was also sceptical about the evolution of inferior races, based his pessimism in *La Psychologie ethnique* on the 'fact' that black Africans primarily exhibited the traits found among children in the more developed races.[19] He drew his proof of the primitive mentality and childlike nature of Africans from the evidence of travellers, missionaries and ethnographers. His starting point was the stereotype of the African's incapacity for abstraction which he embellished with the allegation that the black was also unable to generalise or systematise. He pointed to African language itself as a demonstration of inferiority, explaining: 'First and foremost, the Negro does not like to gather consonants together, so most of the words and syllables in his languages end in vowels—just one more childish characteristic.'[20] Furthermore, he argued that

Africans were as overly loquacious and as addicted to figurative language as children.

Morally, the African was completely a creature of the moment, pre–occupied with immediate self–gratification without regrets about the past or anxieties about the future.[21] His emotional life manifested only fleeting moods; even the love between black mothers and their children was short–lived:

> . . . and like the animals, the mother love of Negresses seems to be of short duration, lasting only until the child knows more and can bring himself up all alone, at his own risk taking on all of life's experiences, dangerous or not.[22]

Extending his inquiry into the realm of African adult relationships, he pronounced them expressions of raw sexual drive, rarely mitigated by tenderness or affection. He subsequently accused African languages of possessing no word for 'love'—at least not love as known and practised by the 'civilised' races.

By 1910, Lucien Lévy–Bruhl was fully convinced that the *modus operandi* of the primitive mind could only be described as one of 'prelogical mentality'.[23] He contended that this process was universal among all primitive peoples, for—no matter how diverse their environment or geographical location—their institutions, ceremonies, beliefs, myths and birth and burial customs were all based upon the mental fusion of things concrete and abstract into a mystical reality. He designated the major characteristics of prelogical mentality as: an unquestioning attitude, a slight tendency to analyse, an incapacity to be modified by experience, an insensibility to contradiction, and (in opposition to Letourneau) a propensity to generalise. Prelogical mentality concerned itself principally with the relationship between objects and the spiritual force or power within them. Thus, for the primitive, the world of the invisible was contained within that of the visible, constantly acting upon it according to the 'law of participation'.[24] For example, before a hunting expedition tribesmen were obliged to perform special rites, including a symbolic capture of game, to cause the presence of animals in the forest during the actual hunt.

After citing many other illustrations of the effect of prelogical mentality on tribal life, language, institutions and beliefs, Lévy–Bruhl concluded that:

(1) The institutions, practices and beliefs of 'primitive' people imply a prelogical and mystical mentality, which is oriented differently from our own.

(2) The collective representations and the relationships between these representations which constitute this mentality are controlled by the law of participation, and as such are indifferent to the logical law of contradiction.[25]

Despite these differences, he regarded the evolution from a prelogical to a logical mentality as a possible but lengthy process.[26]

Lévy–Bruhl's prominence as a scholar endowed his theories with considerable influence at home and abroad, especially among individuals engaged in French colonialism.[27] By inundating his readers with detailed supporting evidence, he obscured from them—as well as himself until his later recantation—the fact that he had really labelled different philosophical premises as different mental functions.[28] Boas, who faulted the Frenchman for studying tribal beliefs and customs rather than individual behaviour, claimed that:

> It would seem that if we disregard the thinking of the individual in our society and pay attention only to current beliefs that we should reach the conclusion that the same attitudes prevail among ourselves that are characteristic of primitive man.[29]

Jean Finot, the editor of the *Revue des revues*, demonstrated the fallacies of viewing race as the dominant factor in human development by citing scientific evidence against racist theories in his book *Le préjugé des races* (1905). Calling the doctrine of racial purity a myth, he stated that, 'if any race is deemed pure from all mixture, it is only because we are unable to disentangle its constituent elements'.[30] He dispelled stereotypes about black physical, mental and moral inferiority by pointing to achievements made by individual blacks in the United States. His final conclusions, despite their cultural chauvinism, were noteworthy because they did not attribute white civilisation to racial determinism:

> ... there are no inferior and superior races, but only races and peoples living outside or within the influence of culture. The appearance of civilisation and its evolution among certain White peoples and within a certain geographical latitude is only the

effect of circumstances. The Negroes, wrongly considered as occupying for ever one of the lowest rungs on the ladder of humanity, bring, by the fact of their raising themselves to the level of the most civilised Whites, a powerful argument in favour of the equality of human capabilities.[31]

Essentially Finot was an advocate of cultural assimilation, confirming potential rather than actual equality between blacks and whites.

Books written before the turn of the century by missionaries and explorers, such as l'Abbé Bouche and Louis–Gustave Binger, considerably influenced the French image of Africans. L'Abbé Bouche, a missionary who served seven years in Dahomey and on the Slave Coast, assumed a monogenist stance in his account of his experiences, declaring that all men belonged to the same general species composed of different races.[32] Seemingly without intentional contradiction, the cleric simultaneously insisted on equality and recognised deficiency, asserting on the one hand that 'The Negro lacks nothing which makes up human nature: his physical organism is the same as that of the white; both of them have the same intellectual and moral faculties'[33]; and on the other that blacks were more intuitive than reflective: emotionally volatile; lacking in foresight, energy, and curiosity; pleasure seeking, and morally sluggish to the point of animalism.[34] Particularly concerned with Dahomean customs, Bouche described them with unusual detachment and conscientiousness until his sensational chapter on human sacrifice. Ironically this chapter undermined all of his pleas for the European acceptance of the human dignity of blacks, becoming the major source for journalists in their coverage of African 'barbarism' during the French conquest of Dahomey (1892–3).[35]

In terms of the popular press, the French involvement in Dahomey was the most important event that moulded public opinion during the first phase of French imperialism.[36] The custom that most fascinated the public was that of human sacrifice—a practice reserved for royalty to insure the purification and atonement of the kingdom. It was exploited, according to Campion–Vincent, to create a mythical image of Dahomey in which the forces of savagery were pitted against those of French culture.[37] The press viewed human sacrifice as so essential to the life of the royal court at Abomey that wars were fought purely for the procurement of sacrificial victims. Recent studies have made a case for the exceptional nature of the 1860 'Great Customs', suggesting that King Ghezo's death was particularly ignoble, caused either by smallpox or murder away from the palace, and thereby necessitated greater sacrifices than usual. Journalists had missed the point that such a death represented a social and spiritual crisis for the Dahomeans who had sought through increased sacrifices of war prisoners and criminals both to appease the angry gods and swell the ranks of Ghezo's army in the afterlife.

What the press derived from l'Abbé Bouche was really graphic detail, for the stereotypes of African brutality, inhumanity, and superstition expressed in their articles were all present in the work of Gobineau and even earlier racist theorists. The French coverage of the Conquest of Dahomey acted more to reinforce an old image rather than create a new one of black Africans.

During this same period, Louis–Gustave Binger achieved renown in France for his explorations of the Upper Niger River and the Ivory Coast. Although in his two–volume account of these expeditions, *Du Niger au Golfe de Guinée par le pays de Kong et le Mossi* (1892), he offered a generally objective description of specific ethnic groups, he occasionally indulged in sweeping statements about blacks. For example, he accused them of an extreme propensity for despotism which necessitated both French intervention and 'direct rule', since Africans should not be given jurisdiction over populous regions.[38] While he did not believe in cannibalism as a current or even a common practice in the past, his recurrent fantasies about it imply the pervasiveness of the European association of the African with it:

> Every time we succeeded in killing a large game animal, the butchering and preparation of the meat always gave rise to the same scenes of cannibalism and savagery among my blacks. It is then that they demonstrate what they really are, for their savage instincts reappear and they resemble brutes rather than human beings.[39]

Binger also invoked the stereotypes of laziness, improvidence and childishness, citing as other deficiencies: an inferiority in mathematical computation, a lack of responsibility, a lack of patriotism proved by the nonexistence of flags among Africans, and an extraordinary cowardice.[40] However, he emphatically credited his men with all the qualities of good servants, 'I myself can affirm that my blacks served me with self–denial and devotion without ulterior motives of self–interest or profit'.[41]

Binger claimed that African infants suffered from severe stimulus deprivation, as a result of being wrapped and carried on their mothers' backs, which retarded their mental growth until they were old enough to walk and run on their own.[42] They then caught up with and experienced the same mental development as European children until the age of puberty, when intellectual growth ceased and the already developed mental powers declined. Without explaining the cause of this mental degeneration, Binger correlated it with the appearance of foolishness, vanity, suspicion, prevarication, and the physical termination of cranial expansion.

Binger had little use for the half–educated Africans, whose excessive affectation, he claimed, was the source of anti–African prejudice.[43] He praised instead the venerable elders who had maintained traditional ways as models of honesty, gravity, good sense and sound judgment. He discounted the ideal of rapidly bringing the African up to the level of the European, regarding *la mission civilisatrice* as a gradual by–product of commercial development rather than an end in itself.[44]

Essentially both l'Abbé Bouche and Binger acknowledged the two major literary images that the nineteenth century had inherited from the eighteenth: *le bon nègre* and *le mauvais nègre*.[45] Binger, the imperialist, however amplified *le bon nègre* to include the African as a large child and *le mauvais nègre* to include the partially Westernised 'native'.

One of the main tenets of French colonial policy was social and political assimilation which, according to Léopold de Saussure, presupposed that races differed from each other mainly as a result of education, and advocated instruction as a method of compensation: 'let us teach the children our language and inculcate them with our ideas and France will soon count by the million, if not new citizens, at least faithful and grateful subjects'.[46] He identified the French predilection for assimilation as a legacy from the reign of Louis XV, for it represented extensions of the Enlightenment principles of the moral unity of mankind and the amelioration of the human race through pure reason.[47] Saussure found these ideas inapplicable to the realities of imperialism, arguing that assimilation through education, institutions and language was a superficial means of training the intellect instead of the character of a race.[48] To him, like Binger, economic development of the colonies would eventually transform 'native' societies without the artificiality of assimilation.⁴⁹

Anti-assimilationist thinking, coupled with the empiricism of such Frenchmen as Maurice Delafosse who had served in the colonies, soon prompted the doctrine of association which stressed the utilisation and recognition of traditional institutions such as the chieftaincy system as well as the creation of new institutions, unlike French ones, tailored to fit the unique needs of the colony. Even though association which allowed for 'indirect rule' stood in sharp contrast to the 'direct rule' of assimilation, both systems perceived French colonialism as permanent rather than temporary. In theory, the ultimate goal of assimilation was the creation of black Frenchmen, but in practice only those Africans born in one of the *Quatres Communes* of Senegal enjoyed full French citizenship of right until the passage of the *Loi Lamine Gueye* on 7 May 1946. Prior to this law the Africans who were not *citoyens* were considered *sujets*, legally covered not by the French Code but the *Indigénat* which greatly restricted their civil rights.

After the First World War the French Colonial Minister (1920–4) Albert Sarraut, who is often compared with Lord Lugard, not only emphasised a functional cooperation between the French administrators and the 'native' elite, but also proposed the establishment of massive economic aid programmes for the development of colonial resources. He advocated the development of medical, educational and agricultural services as a means of elevating the African standard of living, explaining that the metropole could no longer think solely in terms of self-interest:

> ... it is no longer, as it was in the beginning, 'the right of the strongest', but rather 'the right of the strong to help the weakest' which seems to be the noblest and highest right of all.⁵⁰

The realities of the colonies themselves, according to Delavignette, compromised and contradicted both assimilation and association.⁵¹ A certain amount of empiricism prevailed as a consequence of the African and French reactions to each other, so that colonial institutions were actually 'determined by the evolution of the natives in a new African world, rather than by the theoretical conceptions of the home country'.⁵² Race relations in the colonies were marred by French aloofness and superiority, since colonists tended to congregate in urban areas in European enclaves that were distinctly bourgeois, conservative, self-sufficient and exclusive.⁵³ As a safeguard against living and working totally in a European sphere, Delavignette recommended that members of the Colonial Service 'keep one day in the week free from the colonials and entirely devoted to the native, not counting the days spent on tour in the bush'.[54] He credited colonialists with a tolerance for African religions, but an intolerance for African workers who were generally regarded as manpower rather than men.[55]

A more specific catalogue of colonialists' attitudes towards Africans was compiled by René Maunier who studied race relations in the colonies from both the European and African viewpoints.[56] He discovered that cultural conflicts were responsible for the traits that irritated colonialists and confirmed their stereotypes of Africans, noting:

> The white, in the first place, reproaches the coloured man with his *familiarity* and his equality. In the tribe all men are equal; there, a man is always a man: each is of the same blood and of the same rank: in the black man's mind, a black man is as good as a white; the white man believes he has stumbled against an obstacle . . . a failure to appreciate his superiority. He also reproaches the coloured man with his *instability*, his *emotionalism*, his *impulsiveness* which make relations with him extremely insecure . . . The primitive man is quick to change his mind. He is different today than yesterday, you can never count on him.[57]

Maunier also observed that Europeans accused Africans of unreliability and incompetence as part of the older stereotypes of Africans as moral and mental inferiors. Although the alleged undependability was based on the Africans' failure to honour contracts, Maunier explained that the concept of an individual contract was culturally alien to them, for the collectivity of tribal society had never necessitated such agreements.

As a result of his sociological study, Maunier concluded that colonialism as an agent of change would some day raise nationalistic aspirations which would lead to self–government— 'the tragedy of all expansion'.[58] In this insight Maunier was well ahead of his time, for in conducting a survey of members of the French Colonial Service, Cohen found that only by 1958 were 90 per cent of his subjects convinced of the necessity of decolonisation.[59] A year before the Brazzaville Conference (1944) redefined the relationship between France and her black African colonies and called for greater African political participation, Général Paul Azan confidently wrote that the question of independence had not yet arisen because 'the native is happy and proud to belong to the French mother country'.[60]

Even more significant than Azan's assessment of African pride was his description of blacks:

> If one tries to characterise all Blacks, he can say that they have remained very primitive—that they are 'large children'. They love gaiety, laughter and noise, the drums that accompany dances and songs, and long palavers that develop into endless discussions. They are fetishists and when they are Islamised they are only superficially converted, for the memory and the power of the ancestors continue to dominate them.[61]

In addition, he compared the Pygmies to monkeys and claimed that certain unspecified ethnic groups had been cannibals in the not too distant past.[62] He finally concluded that all blacks, no matter how advanced their tribe, were animistic and indolent.

Martine Astier Loutfi has noted that colonisers leaving France around the end of the nineteenth century were influenced by the works of Stanley, Darwin, Nietzche and Kipling, as well as Pierre Loti's *Roman d'un spahi* (1881).[63] With the advent of colonialism, she explains, the genre of the 'exotic' novel, which had been highly refined, ethereal and romantic at the beginning of the nineteenth century, moved away from the esoteric to the popular in 'a vast undertaking of popularisation'.[64] Thus, the images of Africa and Africans in these novels served not only to familiarise the public with current attitudes, but also to convince them of the validity, or occasionally the folly, of colonialism.

Pierre Loti, an opponent of colonialism, so captured the popular imagination that between the years 1880–1900 many young people left for the colonies as a result of reading his novels, especially *Roman d'un spahi*.[65] In 1891 Loti had earned sufficient esteem within the French literary establishment to be elected over Emile Zola to membership in the Académie française. He has been credited by Fanoudh-Siefer with formulating the twentieth century literary image of Africa and hailed by Roland Lebel as the father of French exoticism dealing with black Africa.[66]

The plot of the *Roman d'un spahi* centres around Jean Peyral, a young French soldier stationed in Senegal, who as a consequence of the oppressive heat and hostile landscape falls under the beguiling and enslaving spell of Fatou-gaye, a beautiful Khassonké girl in Saint Louis. Throughout the novel Loti, as a master of 'local colour', portrays Africa as antithetical to European life and Africans as inferior to members of the 'pure' white race. Senegal, as a symbol for all of sub-Saharan Africa, assumes the force of a character, acting more strongly upon Jean than any individual in the story. Except for Jean's one tour in the forested Casamance, Africa is a hot, dry, desolate continent that enervates and debilitates. By painting it as a land of exile in which Europeans feel imprisoned and isolated, Loti makes his opposition to colonialism unmistakable; Jean's death in battle is that of a victim of expansion, not a conqueror.

In Loti's descriptions of Africans only non-Negroid features are associated with beauty. He portrays the two Africans most closely associated with Jean: his friend Nyaor-fall, a black spahi, and his mistress Fatou-gaye respectively as:

> ... an African giant of the magnificent Fouta-Diallonké race with a remarkably impressive face, a fine Arab profile and a mystical smile permanently on his thin lips. He was a handsome statue in black marble.[67]

and

> ... the regularity of Fatou-gaye's features was striking. She was the Khassonké ethnic type in all of its purity with her delicate little Greek face, skin as smooth and black as polished onyx, sparkling white teeth, and an extreme liveliness in her eyes ... (p. 50)

Loti's comparison of the comely black to a statue in marble, ebony or onyx eventually became a stock metaphor in French colonial literature.

Blacks with Negroid features, especially prognathism, are ugly and ape-like. The first Senegalese in the novel are canoers with 'gorilla faces' and Jean's initial impression of Africans is that they all look alike with 'the same monkey mask' (pp. 3, 102). Loti applies the word 'monkey' to blacks more frequently than any other term, even using it with Fatou-gaye whose pink palms at first revolt Jean, creating for him 'an unpleasant, cold sensation of monkey paws' (p. 164). Later on when he has overcome his repulsion, he fondly gives her a Wolof nickname meaning 'little monkey girl' (p. 165). Jean consistently regards his mistress as a house–pet as part of the image of the black woman as a domestic but sexual animal which Loti also contributed to French literature. Loti's assessment of Fatou-gaye's character is really a summary of the traits conventionally associated with 'bad' and 'good' Negroes:

> For a long time Jean had known that little Fatou was deceitful and told lies with an incredible amount of malice and perversity. But he was also aware of the absolute devotion which she had for him—the devotion of a dog for its master—the adoration of a Negro for his fetish . . . (p. 179)

When she is not with Jean, she seeks to perpetuate her spell over him by purchasing charms and amulets from the local *marabouts*. Loti, who claims that Jean for one moment 'almost loved' Fatou-gaye, makes it eminently clear throughout the novel that Jean's attraction to her is a result of the combined effects of her evil machinations and the hellish environment (p. 157). She is so successful because she herself is a product of this intolerable climate and landscape—a 'succulent fruit of the Soudan, ripened precociously by the tropical springtime, swollen with toxic juices, filled with unhealthy, feverish and exotic sensual pleasures . . .' (p. 115).

In dealing with the other Africans in the book, Loti generally emphasises their odour, incapability to love (since they buy and sell wives), monkey–like sensuality, cruelty, songs and dances. The only positive attribute he assigns to Africans is a love of homeland: 'Negroes have a love for their village, their tribe, and the piece of earth where they were born' (p. 128).

Loti's low opinion of racial mixtures is evident in his portrayal of Cora, a mulatto, whose abuse of Jean's innocent affection begins the spahi's personal dissipation. The unnaturalness of racial crossing is even protested by Jean's infant mulatto son, who 'did not want his mother's blood' since it fused his 'pure' French blood with that of the 'impure black race' (pp. 308–9). During the temporary separation which occurs between Jean and Fatou–gaye, more than anything else he feels a resurgence of his racial dignity and pride:

> It seemed to him, moreover, that he had regained his dignity as a white man, which had been sullied by his contact with Fatou's black flesh. His former intoxication—the fever of senses over-

stimulated by the African climate—enflamed him no longer, and when he looked back over his life, he felt a profound disgust. (p. 263).

The images of Africans which Pierre Loti favoured in the *Roman d'un spahi* were largely derived from educated French belief in the inequality of races and the evils of racial hybridism. The popularity of the novel soon turned Fatou–gaye and the anonymous blacks in the story into stock characters in subsequent colonial novels. Loti's work proved seminal for both those authors who accepted and those who rejected his view of Africans, since dissenting writers tended to draw characters diametrically opposed to his. His treatment of the black woman was widely imitated, making her, in the opinion of Loutfi, the most popular African character in colonial novels between the years 1881–1914, followed by the African in the process of assimilation.[68] The colonial novels read for this study reveal that these two characters have prevailed in literature from the end of the First World War through the mid-1960s as well.

The French emphasis on the black woman, often with the idea of encountering the 'soul of the people' through her, has no real counterpart in British colonial literature. The dearth of black women as mistresses in British novels may be a function of Victorian prudery and of the celebrated pluck of English women who accompanied their husbands in the Colonial service to the field from an earlier date and in greater numbers than did French wives. The social colour bar thoroughly 'white–washed' the romantic novel, making plots largely centre around young, dashing officers whose sweethearts were the visiting relatives of other English colonialists. However, when African women did appear, the British largely restricted their roles to those of a human drudge, slaving away while the men slept, or a sex object for the pleasure of Englishmen.

In French literature, even though the black woman was sometimes considered superior to black men, she served primarily as a sex object—the 'bush wife' of a Frenchman. Ada Martinkus–Zemp has demonstrated that only the Fulbe women of the West African Sudan escaped this reduction to female objects, since they were regarded as half-way between the refinement of French women and the animalism of black ones.[69] Authors concentrated on their faces, features, amber complexion and bright wrappers, but black women were perceived as naked bodies without faces whose beauty was solely based on their breasts and thighs. Partially due to

Loti's treatment of Fatou–gaye, black mistresses were presented either as statues or house–pets, while Fulbe women were compared to graceful antelope or deer. Quite often in these works, European men suffered severe disappointment, for the erotic promise they had falsely ascribed to black women was not fulfilled in sexual relations because of the passivity and uninvolvement of their mistresses.

The only consistently positive black male figure was the black soldier in the French armed services. Here again a direct line of descent can be traced from the *Roman d'un spahi*, for Jean's closest friend was Nyaor–fall, a black spahi. Although many novels portrayed black members of the Senegalese Sharpshooters as loyal, courageous and well–mannered, only a few authors explicitly stated that these qualities were the result of the French influence blacks encountered in the service. A number of novels, especially those written before the large scale drafting of Africans to serve in the French forces in the First World War, gave the distinct impression that these men were much finer than civilian blacks. Authors, nevertheless, continued to highlight their superstitions, fetishes, dances and songs in much the same manner as Pierre Loti.

The character of the partially educated African provides the greatest degree of consensus in French and British colonial literature, since he was nearly unanimously ridiculed and scorned for being arrogant, pretentious and imitative. In French novels an author's attitude towards a particular colonial philosophy pivoted around this character. For writers who endorsed the policy of assimilation, Africans who refused to assimilate and fought to remain 'savage' justified colonial domination, while novelists who disagreed with this doctrine showed that Africans who tried to assimilate were ludicrous from either the French or the African vantage point. In either case the French colonial presence was validated, because the 'primitives' needed civilising and the 'large children' needed guidance.

The French portrayal of house boys, interpreters and clerks greatly emphasised language, clothing and reversion. It must be remembered that one of the basic principles of assimilation was the teaching of French, so it followed that individuals who had received some education yet still spoke vulgarised French reinforced the concept of African inferiority and mental deficiency. As for the African adoption of European clothing, most authors condemned it when it went much beyond the garb necessary for 'decency'—

trousers, shirts and dresses. Reversion was presented as the proof that most of an African's Westernisation was strictly superficial and could easily be effaced upon returning to a traditional village. It was not unusual for *évolués* in many novels to resort to witchcraft or participate in 'pagan' rites when they were beset with problems or visited relatives in the 'bush'.

A subdivision of the novel of the *évolué* which mainly appeared after 1918 was that of the colonised viewed by himself—a novel in which a French author assumed the African point of view, sometimes using the technique of a black narrator.[70] Once again, as in the case of the black woman, this subgenre has no substantial analogue in British colonial literature set in West Africa. A fair amount of ethnographic material dealing with language and customs was incorporated into a number of these works to insure authenticity, while others concentrated on African stereotypes of Europeans as a means of satirising whites in the colonies. Most of these books were fairly unconvincing, tending merely to confirm stock images from a different angle.

French colonial novels in the twentieth century have preserved most of Pierre Loti's literary formulations of nineteenth century African stereotypes, revealing the same process of transfer observed in twentieth century British colonial literature. The specific stereotypes which permeate both literatures correlate to such a significant degree that they are considered together in the following chart of stereotypes most often encountered in British and French background materials and colonial novels.

EUROPEAN STEREOTYPES OF AFRICANS

AFRICANS IN GENERAL

Physically, are:

1 ugly, monkey-like, all look alike
2 bad-smelling
3 sensually acute

Mentally, are:

1 deficient, incompetent, ignorant, unlettered, uncultured
2 unable to think abstractly
3 imitative (partially educated African is the worst)

Morally, are:

1 superstitious, heathen, primitive, savage
2 demonic, evil, cruel, unpitying, cannibalistic
3 large children, happy-go-lucky, undependable, lacking in sense of duty and foresight, cowardly, always late, lazy
4 deceitful, covetous, liars and thieves
5 vain, ungrateful
6 oversexed, animalistic, copulate but do not make love
7 good (faithful) servants and soldiers

Emotionally, are:

1 unable to show emotion
2 impulsive, unstable, ruled by passions and moods
3 good dancers and singers

AFRICANS IN PARTICULAR

African men are:

1 unambitious, let women do all the work
2 endowed with large sexual organs, desirous of raping white women
3 disrespectful of black women because of polygamy, wife buying and selling

African women are:

1 drudges, beasts of burden
2 sex objects (French variation of the black woman as domestic animal)
3 unresponsive, poor lovers

Mulattoes are:

1 impure, unnatural, undesirable
2 scorned, rejected by either race
3 cunning, crafty

NOTES

1. Arendt, p. 172. Curtin, p. 381. Cohen, p. 185.
2. Curtin, pp. 367-8, 379, 381.
3. Curtin, p. 378. Arendt, p. 172.
4. Arthur de Gobineau, *Essai sur l'inégalité des races humaines* (Paris: Editions Belfond, 1967. First published, vol. i–ii, 1853; complete version, vol. i–iv, 1855) p. 205.
5. Ibid., p. 24. Translation is mine.
6. Ibid., pp. 77, 205-6.

7. Michael D. Biddiss, *Father of Racist Ideology: The Social and Political Thought of Count Gobineau* (New York: Weybright and Talley, 1970) p. 117.
8. Ibid., p. 119.
9. Alfred Fouillée, 'Le Caractère des races humaines et l'avenir de la race blanche', *Revue des deux Mondes*, cxxiv, No. 4 (July-Aug. 1894) p. 90. Translation is mine.
10. Ibid., pp. 82, 88–90.
11. Ibid., p. 90. Translation is mine.
12. Ibid., pp. 103, 91.
13. Gustave LeBon, *The Psychology of Peoples* (New York: Macmillan, 1898) p. 24. Translator not given.
14. Ibid., p. 27.
15. Ibid., p. 29.
16. Ibid., pp. 29–30.
17. Ibid., p. 37.
18. Gobineau, p. 183.
19. Charles Letourneau, *La Psychologie ethnique* (Paris: Schleicher Frères, Editeurs, 1901) pp. 117, 126–8.
20. Ibid., p. 126. Translation is mine.
21. Ibid., pp. 112, 114.
22. Ibid., p. 112. Translation is mine.
23. Lucien Lévy-Bruhl, *Les Fonctions mentales dans les sociétés inférieures* (Paris: Librairie Félix Alcan, 1928; first published 1910) pp. 79; 6, 67; 16, 113–4, 136; 127; 263.
24. Ibid., p. 76. Translation is mine.
25. Ibid., p. 127. Translation is mine.
26. Ibid., p. 447.
27. Robert Delavignette, *Freedom and Authority in French West Africa*, trans. by Prof. M. Fortes, Miss Daphne Trevor, and Miss. M. Manoukian (London: Oxford Univ. Press, 1950) p. 39.
28. In 1938 he retracted the idea of 'primitive mentality' in notes that were published posthumously in his *Carnets* (1949).
29. Boas, *The Mind of Primitive Man*, p. 128.
30. Jean Finot, *Race Prejudice*, trans. by Florence Wade–Evans (London: Archibald Constable & Co. Ltd., 1906) pp. 157, 319.
31. Ibid., p. 308.
32. L'Abbé Pierre Bouche, *La Côte des Esclaves et le Dahomey* (Paris: E. Plon, Nourrit et Cie, Imprimeurs-Editeurs, 1885) p. 16.
33. Ibid., p. 16. Translation is mine.
34. Ibid., pp. 23–5.
35. Véronique Campion–Vincent, 'L'Image du Dahomey dans la presse française (1890–1895): les sacrifices humains', *Cahiers d'Etudes Africaines*, vol. vii, no. 25 (1967) pp. 41–2. L'Abbé Bouche's account of the 1860 sacrifices which he had not witnessed was convenient for journalists because he quoted extensively from the early 1860s versions of Lartique and Borghero and described illustrations published in 1878 in *Missions Catholiques*.
36. See Richard Lee Smith, 'The Image of West Africa in the French Mass Press, 1876–1909' (diss. Rutgers Univ., 1972) pp. 64–9, for a tabulation of the total number of articles dealing with West Africa in two tabloid newspapers, *Le Petit*

Journal and *Le Petit Parisien*. By 1892 Dahomey was the most publicised story of the year with *Le Petit Journal* covering it 140 times and *Le Petit Parisien* 189 times. Articles on Dahomey continued through 1895, turning General Dobbs into 'the Vanquisher of Behanzin' in adventure story copy.
37. Campion–Vincent, pp. 27–31, 40–5, 55–6.
38. Capitaine Louis-Gustave Binger, *Du Niger au Golfe de Guinée par le pays de Kong et le Mossi*, vols. i and ii (Paris: Librairie Hachette, 1892) vol. i, p. 153.
39. Ibid., vol. ii, p. 7. Translation is mine.
40. Ibid., pp. 214, 245–6.
41. Ibid., p. 246. Translation is mine.
42. Ibid., p. 246.
43. Ibid., p. 246.
44. Ibid., pp. 347–8.
45. Léon Fanoudh-Siefer, *Le Mythe du nègre et de l'Afrique noire dans la littérature française (de 1800 à la 2e Guerre Mondiale)* (Paris: Librairie C. Klincksieck, 1968) pp. 40–1.
46. Léopold de Saussure, *Psychologie de la Colonisation française dans ses rapports avec les sociétés indigènes* (Paris: Ancienne Librairie Germer Baillière et Cie, Félix Alcan, Editeur, 1899) pp. 10, 27–8. Trans. is mine.
47. Ibid., p. 31.
48. Ibid., pp. 47–51, 53, 110, 134, 162, 165.
49. Ibid., p. 258.
50. Albert Sarraut, *Grandeur et servitude coloniales* (Paris: Editions du Sagittaire, 1931) p. 115. Translation is mine.
51. Delavignette, p. 49.
52. Ibid., p. 51.
53. Ibid., pp. 16, 18, 20.
54. Ibid., p. 33.
55. Ibid., p. 37.
56. René Maunier, *The Sociology of Colonies: An Introduction to the Study of Race Contact*, ed. and trans. by E. O. Lorimer, vols. i and ii (London: Routledge & Kegal Paul Ltd., 1949; first published, 1932–42) pp. 82–3.
57. Ibid., pp. 82–3.
58. Ibid., p. 418.
59. William B. Cohen, *Rulers of Empire: The French Colonial Service in Africa* (Palo Alto: Hoover Institution Press, Stanford Univ., 1971) pp. 188–92. The older men in his sample tended to ascribe the independence drive to 'outside international forces', while younger ones attributed it to nationalistic ones within the colonies.
60. Général Paul Azan, *L'Empire français* (Paris: Flammarion, Editeur, 1943) p. 230. Translation is mine.
61. Ibid., pp. 81–3. Translation is mine.
62. Ibid., pp. 82–3.
63. Martine Astier Loutfi, *Littérature et colonialisme: l'expansion coloniale vue dans la littérature romanesque française 1871–1914* (The Hague: Mouton, 1971) pp. 45, 50, 58, 113–14.
64. Ibid., p. 44. Translation is mine.
65. Ibid., p. 50.
66. Cohen, 'Literature and Race . . .', pp. 19, 49. Roland Lebel, *Histoire de la*

littérature coloniale en France (Paris: Librairie Larose, 1931) p. 70.
67. Pierre Loti, *Le Roman d'un spahi* (Paris: Calmann–Lévy, Éditeurs, n.d.; vol. 8 of his *Oeuvres*) p. 38. All subsequent page references will be to this edition, and will follow immediately in the text. This translation and all subsequent ones are my own.
68. Loutfi, p. 61.
69. Ada Martinkus-Zemp, 'Européocentrisme et exotisme: l'homme blanc et la femme noire (dans la littérature française de l'entre deux-guerres)', *Cahiers d'Etudes Africaines*, vol. xiii, No. 49 (1972) pp. 62, 64–7, 70–5, 79.
70. Loutfi, p. 137.

3 Stereotypes Preserved: *A Yellow Napoleon*, *The Heart of the Matter*, *Batouala*, and *Koffi*

The four novels included in this chapter: *A Yellow Napoleon* (1928) *The Heart of the Matter* (1948), *Batouala* (1921) and *Koffi* (1922) will be analysed in terms of the racial stereotypes that their authors reinforce in their creation of African characters. While the works have not been arranged as a chronology of British or French colonial history, the fixed images of Africans they present do reflect the racial attitudes that prevailed in both colonial society and novels until the emergence of black nationalism after the Second World War.

Although the literary merits of these works by Arthur E. Southon, Graham Greene, René Maran and Gaston Joseph, respectively, far exceed those of many colonial novels, only Greene and Maran have achieved the status of recognised writers. Southon, a missionary who romanticised his experiences in novels, and Joseph, a French colonial officer who only wrote one work of fiction, remain in obscurity. The fact that each of these authors came to west or Central Africa—namely to Nigeria, Sierra Leone, Central African Republic and the Ivory Coast—in different professional capacities has influenced the settings of their novels far more than their characterisation of Africans. All of them have largely cast Africans into the familiar categories of 'good' and 'bad' natives, whether they are endorsing or condemning colonialism.

Rev. Arthur Eustace Southon, a Methodist missionary in Western Nigeria from 1911 to 1915, combines melodrama with didacticism in *A Yellow Napoleon* to illustrate the nobleness of the missionary cause. Set in a remote area of Nigeria, his novel portrays the colonial era after 1900 but before the First World War. The only substantial efforts to develop this area come, in keeping with

Southon's bias, from missionary rather than government projects.

The title of the novel pertains to the main character Tulasi and comes from the stereotypes of the half—caste as an anathema to Africans and Europeans alike. Quite predictably the villain is a mulatto, since a black one would undermine his contention that 'benighted' Africans welcome the opportunity to 'upgrade' themselves through Christianity.

In the plot Tulasi, the son of an Irish reprobate and his Nigerian mistress, develops a thorough hatred for both Europeans and Africans because of their refusal to accept him. After a fight with a white man in Lagos, he flees to 'the Rogues' Refuge' in Mperu where he becomes the leader of a band of criminals. He ascends to power by inventing the god Mimba–Karo who supposedly will enable the blacks to drive out the whites and create an African empire. His plans for revolt are thwarted by the British Commissioner Harley Fane and his Hausa Police Guards, who surprise Tulasi at a ritual of human sacrifice, wound him in his Mimba–Karo disguise, and expose his religion as a hoax. In revenge Tulasi, who is thought to have died, re–establishes the worship of Mimba–Karo through the agency of his Mperu thieves as a secret men's society called the 'Brotherhood of Death'. This time both man and nature conquer Tulasi, for after Fane destroys the Brotherhood a mahogany tree fatally crushes the mulatto.

In addition, the novel contains two romantic subplots involving two sets of lovers: Makindi, the nephew of the Shango priestess, and Feribo—'the Flower of Kwandi', the daughter of the king; and Frank Rilston, the first Christian missionary in Kwandi, and Mildred Fane, the sister of Harley Fane. The author carefully balances the vicissitudes of each courtship, for in both cases changes in belief and attitude must occur before the couples may marry.

In drawing Tulasi, Makindi, Feribo and the Shango priestess Nadu, Southon relies on both action and explanation. While the characters reveal themselves through deeds and dialogue, the author's judgments and intrusions inform us of their inner thoughts. Indeed, he approaches his characters as an overexplanatory puppeteer who constantly interprets as well as controls.

Tulasi, as a result of his mixed parentage, represents a duality of mental and emotional powers that epitomises the white supremacist assessment of Europeans and Africans:

On his mental side he was of a higher order than the natives, but on the emotional he was pure African and savage . . .

Two men lived under the skin of Tulasi; one thinking, sensitive, highly gifted person, the produce of centuries of social evolution, the other a primitive creature made up of crude emotions, the product of centuries of savagery.[1]

Although Southon takes this dichotomy as a text for his authorial comments about Tulasi's malice and cunning, he never permits the mulatto as a character to express the dramatic potential of his inner conflict. He primarily treats Tulasi's hostility toward whites as a simple response to their rejection, so the information given in the passages below appears without preparation:

This night it came home to him that it must be one or the other; he must choose between the white and the black within him. In his heart he despised the natives, yet, because of his hatred of the white men who had always spurned him, he decided to throw in his lot for ever with the blacks and use them for his purposes. Instead of cherishing his secret, impossible dream—to be recognised as a white man—he would call himself after this a native of the natives . . .

Beneath those emotional storms his deeper, truer self yearned after his white father's race, and he had cherished a secret but intense delight in the white blood in his veins. (p. 41)

In neglecting to supply sufficient psychological motivation for Tulasi's hatred as frustrated admiration, Southon appears to assume that mulattoes naturally value their white strain more highly than their black one.

According to the author, Tulasi uses religion as his means to power because he knows how easy it is to manipulate black religious fear. Tulasi capitalises on African 'emotional volatility', for in several scenes he produces a state of frenzy with little effort by invoking Mimba–Karo and anti–Europeanism. By the end of the story Tulasi completely reverts to 'savagery' in his conviction that Shango, the god of thunder, has always foiled his plans:

For the moment he was all African. It came upon him that it was not the Commissioner who pursued him so relentlessly, always defeating him when he was within an ace of triumph. It was Shango and all the gods of Africa whom he had outraged by his blasphemy in setting up a rival god in Mimba–Karo. (p. 232)

Tulasi, as 'the half–caste with the brain and overweening egoism of a Napoleon and the hatred of a devil,' embodies several familiar stereotypes of Africans and mulattoes (p. 238). Although his diabolical character results from miscegenation, Southon views his emotionalism and superstition as purely African traits. On the other hand, his success in dominating blacks is ascribed to his European qualities—foresight, intelligence and imagination. The writer constantly directs our attention to the fact that Tulasi is a half–caste, for while mulattoes are always bad to him, black Africans can be good.

Makindi, Feribo and Nadu serve as three outstanding examples of 'good Africans' who come from the literary tradition of 'the noble savage'. Southon particularly stresses the physical, mental and moral attractiveness of the lovers, Makindi and Feribo, who stand apart from 'ordinary' blacks. For example, he writes of Makindi:

> And as the gods had favoured Makindi with a perfect body so they had been generous with his mind. Even a casual glance at his big, flashing eyes, his broad, strong nose with its thin, sensitive nostrils, and the great rock of a jaw, would have told a thoughtful observer that a mind superior to the average dwelt in the large, finely poised head. Makindi was by birth a chief in Kwandi, and by virtue of both mind and body he was unquestionably a chief among men, as inevitably born to lead as an eagle to soar to the clouds. (p. 55)

Southon couches his appraisal of Makindi's mind in relative terms, avoiding the application of the word 'intelligent' to an African. Feribo, because she is half Fulani, approximates European criteria of beauty even more closely:

> Her mother was a Fulani, one of that strange race in Northern Nigeria which claims to be a white people, and which can trace back its history for thousands of years. From her mother Feribo had inherited her perfect figure and features of almost classical beauty, and in colour she was no darker than a Spaniard. Judged by European standards she was a lovely girl and the king idolised her. (p. 48)

During their long courtship Southon uses two moral tests to prove the natural goodness of Makindi and Feribo, who 'would have inspired a sculptor's masterpiece on the Parents of the Race' (p. 57). At the beginning of the novel Feribo, betrothed to a neighbouring king in her infancy, refuses to elope with Makindi, persuading him that they should deny themselves rather than tarnish her father's honour. As a consequence of this righteous but difficult decision, Southon awards the couple his highest compliment:

> And the gods, who ever love those who tread the way of duty, looked down on these two *white-souled* children of a savage land, and smiled. (p. 60; emphasis mine).

The second moral test comes later on when Feribo's father, angered by Makindi's conversion to Christianity, forces him to choose between the white man's religion and his daughter. Greatly tempted by the offer, Makindi decides against his heart in favour of his soul. By the end of the novel Feribo's 'white soul' has accepted Christ and Rilston marries the exemplary couple in the one-thousand member Kwandi Christian Church.

The author draws Nadu, the Shango priestess, as a complex character whose religious ideas conflict with her maternal sentiments. While he paints her 'pagan' side as proud and uncompromising, he shows her maternal one as tender and understanding. When Tulasi usurps her power as Kwandi's chief religious leader, she becomes his only African opponent. Similarly when Rilston begins his missionary activities in Kwandi, she twice attempts to murder him. Southon conveys through Nadu his opinion that African religions base themselves on fear and superstition, fostering only resentment and bitterness. Nadu, the adoptive mother of her nephew, displays a deep love and concern for Makindi. These attributes prevail when Makindi is dying, permitting her to forget her pride and call for medical aid from Rilston. The British missionary's success in saving Makindi's life instills her first doubts about Shango's omnipotence. When she observes the positive changes that Christianity has brought to her nephew, she too worships the white man's God. Yet, even before her conversion, Southon claims that she, like all Africans, secretly admires whites:

> At last she was going to strike a powerful blow for the gods; to strike down a white man, one of that strange race whose innate

superiority she felt in common with all primitive people, but which her pride would not admit. (pp. 170–1)

Although this white supremacist assumption of 'innate superiority' recurs several more times in the story, Southon generally moves a little beyond the stereotypical level in his depiction of Nadu. Unlike Tulasi and the lovers who are monotonous in their evil and goodness respectively, Nadu's combination of strengths and weaknesses engages the reader's sympathy. As a consequence of the author's development of her personal qualities along with her conflicts as a priestess and mother, she emerges as the most credible African in the book.

The most interesting aspect of *A Yellow Napoleon*, however, is the unintentional irony with which the authorial voice undercuts Rilston's assertions that Africans and Europeans are brothers. Apparently Southon found no inconsistency between Christianity and white supremacy, so Rilston's strongest affirmation of black/white fraternity is paternalistic:

> They [Rilston and Makindi] were together for hours every day, and the missionary discovered that in the things which are basal brotherhood is a very real thing. He himself was the product of centuries of social evolution, a cultured scholar, with a mind richly stored with the treasures of the world's hard-won knowledge; Makindi was a true child of Darkest Africa, ignorant, untutored, but a natural gentleman. Constantly Rilston was impressed with the fineness of his feelings and his high standard of honour. His own love for Mildred was no cleaner, better feeling than that of this dark son of Africa for Feribo. (pp. 203–4)

Characteristically Rilston never mentions a meeting of minds, only emotions and spirit, in his respect for Africans.

While Southon may appear to vary from the usual stereotype of Africans as incapable of true love and affection, the long chaste romance of Makindi and Feribo belongs completely to the eighteenth century handling of 'the noble savage'. Furthermore, by insisting that they are exceptional Africans, he insures that the stereotypes applied to 'ordinary' Africans will not be invalidated.

Southon's images of Africans confirm the stereotypes of blacks as childish, inferior creatures of emotion, ignorance, fear, primitiveness and mental deficiency. According to G. D. Killam, the unconvincing portrayal of Africans, the paternalistic tone and white supremacist declarations in *A Yellow Napoleon* make it fully representative of the novels published between 1900 and 1939 which deal with Britain's responsibility to Africans.[2]

One of the most unusual aspects of Graham Greene's *The Heart of the Matter* is the author's inattention to Africans. Based more on Greene's experiences as a British intelligence officer in Freetown from 1942–3 than his Liberian bush travels of 1935, the novel is set in Sierra Leone during the Second World War. Greene focuses on white colonials who largely cling to the same stereotypes of Africans encountered in much earlier colonial novels. If it were not for the references to the war, the world of the novel would seem timelessly colonial, defined by the office, the Club and the colour bar.

While most of the Africans who appear in the book as policemen, servants and whores fall into the stock categories of fearful and dishonest natives, Greene presents Major Scobie's boy Ali as a 'good servant'. In the case of Ali—the only real African character—Greene still depends on stereotypes, yet he raises them from racial into literary symbols. Ali functions as a crucial element in the novel, not because of himself but because of Scobie's relationship with him.

In drawing Ali, Greene has particularly emphasised the boy's devotion to Scobie. The short, squat boy 'with the broad ugly pleasant face of a Temne' appears to have no purpose in life other than serving his master.[3] Ali, who has been with Scobie for fifteen years, has not only always refused offers to work for other employers, but has except for once always met Scobie at the wharf after each furlough. On one occasion Greene develops Ali's waiting for Scobie implicitly as a dog–master faithfulness:

> It was nearly one in the morning before he [Scobie] returned: the light was out in the kitchen quarters and Ali was dozing on the step of the house until the head-lamps woke him, passing across his sleeping face. He jumped up and lit the way from the garage with his torch.
> 'All right, Ali. Go to bed.' (p. 105)

Ali rises above this level of subservience only when he demonstrates his concern for Scobie's health or comfort. At such times he becomes assertive, disagreeing with Scobie and even giving commands. For example, he refuses to put a plaster as requested on the cut on Scobie's hand, since he knows a bandage would provide more protection:

> 'Now the elastoplast'.
> 'No,' Ali said, 'no. Bandage better.'
> 'All right. Bandage then.' Years ago he [Scobie] had taught Ali to Bandage: now he could tie one as expertly as a doctor. (p. 38)

In order to take proper care of Scobie, Ali in this passage assumes the initiative and displays his competence.

During the journey up to Bamba in the police van, the greatest moment of comradeship occurs between them when Ali puts his arm around Scobie's shoulder and hands him a mug of hot tea. This unexpected pleasure reminds Scobie of 'the old days', so he fondly asks Ali:

> 'Do you remember, Ali, that two hundred 002 trek we did twelve years ago in ten days, along the border; two of the carriers went sick. . . .'
> He could see in the driver's mirror Ali nodding and beaming. It seemed to him that this was all he needed of love or friendship. (p. 84)

Ali says nothing during this reminiscence, for as a character he has no personal life of his own; he exists solely as an adjunct to Scobie. By reducing his needs for love and friendship to Ali's nods and smiles, Scobie reveals his high regard for self-containment in human relationships. This definition of love as a mixture of warmth and distance confirms Derek Traversi's contention that Scobie cannot commit himself to others, because that would violate the isolation he prizes.[4] Scobie's pattern of interaction with the boy makes no emotional demands on his solitude.

Scobie's trust in Ali distinguishes him from most of the other Europeans, for until his own acts of deception he views Ali as an embodiment of loyalty. His association of Ali with trust is so fixed, that the boy even appears in Scobie's dream about the friendly snake:

> . . . but when he slept he went smoothly back into a dream of perfect happiness and freedom. He was walking through a wide cool meadow with Ali at his heels: there was nobody else

anywhere in his dream, and Ali never spoke. Birds went by far overhead, and once when he sat down the grass was parted by a small green snake which passed onto his hand and up his arm without fear and before it slid down into the grass again touched his cheek with a cold friendly remote tongue. (p. 82)

Although here a case can certainly be made for Ali's canine devotion to his master, the unfrightened behaviour of the snake points to trust as the larger theme of the dream. The lack of fear on both the part of the snake and Scobie emphasises a mutual faith that neither will be harmed. Ali's presence as the only person with Scobie at the time he handles the snake seems to identify him with this trust along with Scobie's ideal of isolation. The Snake's 'friendly remote tongue', joining friendship with distance, may be the origin of Scobie's later thoughts when he watches Ali in the rearview mirror. Even though Ali's silence conforms to the image of the quiet, obedient servant, it may also manifest his trust in Scobie. The dream reveals a linkage of happiness, freedom, isolation and trust with Ali in Scobie's subconscious mind.

Greene first refers to Scobie's distrust of Ali after the police officer doubts whether he can trust in God's mercy to the woman he abandons. When he interrogates Ali about his brother who works for Mr Wilson, he tries inwardly to argue away his suspicions:

It seemed to Scobie one of the qualities of deceit that you lost the sense of trust. If I can lie and betray, so can others. Wouldn't many people gamble on my honesty and lose their stake? Why should I lose my stake on Ali? I have not been caught and he has not been caught, that's all. An awful depression weighed his head towards the wheel. He thought: I know that Ali is honest: I have known that for fifteen years: I am just trying to find a companion in this region of lies. Is the next stage the stage of corrupting others? (p. 255)

It must be noted that a network of house boys as spies does exist, since Wilson has bribed Yusef's boy and Yusef has bribed Scobie's mistress' boy. However, despite Traversi's and Laitinen's claims, there remains no conclusive proof that Ali has become involved in Wilson's espionage[5]. In the long run such arguments seem unimportant, for Scobie himself makes us perfectly aware in the passage above that he is beginning psychologically to project his deceit onto Ali.

Greene correlates the next incident which arouses Scobie's suspicions even more closely with the policeman's distrust of God. Scobie discovers Ali in the dark garage, where Scobie has just kissed his mistress Helen Rolt shortly after he has resolved not to forsake either her or his wife:

> O God, I can't leave her. Or Louise, You don't need me as they need me. You have your good people, your Saints, all the company of the blessed. You can do without me. (pp. 259–60)

In spite of Ali's explanation and Helen's assurance that he is telling the truth, Scobie finds the boy's presence in the garage disturbing. This time he cannot placate his fears of betrayal:

> 'I've had Ali for fifteen years,' Scobie said. It was the first time he had been ashamed before him in all those years. He remembered Ali the night after Pemberton's death, cup of tea in hand, holding him up against the shaking lorry, and then he remembered Wilson's boy slinking off along the wall by the police station.
> 'You can trust him anyway'. [Helen]
> 'I don't know how' Scobie said, 'I've lost the trick of trust.' (pp. 260–1)

By now Scobie has convinced himself of Ali's disloyalty, since in losing the trick of trusting God, he has also lost the trick of trusting man.

What finally prompts Scobie to confide his distrust of Ali to Yusef is not so much the thought that the boy could ruin Scobie as the fear that he might compromise Helen and Louise. Yusef commiserates with Scobie and claims that he will find out whether Ali can be trusted. Without disclosing his plan, he asks Scobie for a token to send Ali so that the boy will come down to the wharf. Since he is unable to remove his signet ring from his finger, he gives Yusef his broken rosary—a symbol of his broken trust of God. Although Scobie, as an experienced police officer, suspects Yusef's treachery, he never compels Yusef to explain how he will deal with Ali. Ali's death cry finally answers all of the questions Scobie never asked.

When Scobie searches the wharf in the darkness, he seems

instinctively drawn to Ali's body. Upon discovering it, he understands that he was the cause of the murder: 'Didn't I know all the time in Yusef's room that something was planned? Couldn't I have pressed for an answer?' (p. 277). Scobie's last image of Ali draws the correlation between his distrust of God and distrust of Ali so tightly that Ali and God fuse together:

> . . . he saw the body as something very small and dark and a long way away—like a broken piece of the rosary he looked for: a couple of black beads and the image of God coiled at the end of it. O God, he thought, I've killed you: you've served me all these years and I've killed you at the end of them. God lay there under the petrol drums and Scobie felt the tears in his mouth, salt in the cracks of his lips. You served me and I did this to you. You were faithful to me, and I wouldn't trust you.
> 'What is it, sah?' the corporal whispered, kneeling by the body.
> 'I loved him,' Scobie said. (p. 277)

Scobie's confession that he loved Ali acquires great importance, for in a later internal dialogue with God he confesses that he loves God, but does not trust him. During the same discussion, the voice of God pleads, 'Can't you trust me as you'd trust a faithful dog?' suggesting Ali's waiting for Scobie and following on his heels (p. 290). Indeed, Scobie sees himself as the cause of both Ali's and God's suffering. Greene has prepared us for Scobie's response to the corpse in earlier passages where the policeman imagines himself striking the face of God with his fists. To Scobie Ali's death as a victim of his master's sin illustrates in the real world what he is doing to God in the spiritual one.

In coming to the notoriously dangerous wharf at night on the pledge of Scobie's rosary, Ali exhibits complete faith in Scobie and the goodness of his intentions. This act of total fidelity makes him a foil to Scobie, for, unlike his master who arrived at the wharf in distrust, Ali arrives in trust. When Scobie sees Ali's broken body, it incarnates the rosary; the body is now a symbol of his broken faith. Scobie's vision of Ali as God unites in his mind the two things he has most loved and most distrusted.

Graham Greene's treatment of Ali remains an extraordinary example of how an author can simultaneously keep a character as a stereotype on one level and extend him as a literary symbol on another. In *The Heart of the Matter* Greene not only uses the deteriorating relationship between Scobie and Ali as an 'objective correlative' of that between Scobie and God, but finally heightens the 'good servant' in his last act of obedience into a God–figure.

René Maran, the author of *Batouala*, is another professional writer who has created African characters based upon racial stereotypes. A Martinican in the French Colonial Service who absorbed French attitudes during his many years of formal education in France, Maran served in Ubangi–Shari (now the Central African Republic) from 1910 until 1923 when the controversy engendered by *Batouala* pressured him into early retirement. After the novel received the Prix Goncourt in 1921 Maran was the victim of a number of scathing articles, often written by French colonial administrators. These critics, outraged by the success of a work with such anti–European attitudes, accused him of having maligned both the colonisers and the colonised. For example, Governor General Gabriel Angoulvant of the Ivory Coast denounced him for having:

> ... allowed himself, as a Negro, to describe with a particularly cruel pen one of the most backward peoples of Africa, satisfying at the same time in his work his prejudices against the white race to which he does not belong, and his contempt for his racial brothers less evolved than he.[6]

Maran, who spent six years writing and revising *Batouala*, sought to make it an objective depiction of reality. Although Léopold Senghor regards Maran as 'the precursor of Negritude' and credits him with expressing '"the black soul" in the Negro style in French,' the novel with its influence from Flaubert and Zola belongs fully to the French literary tradition of the late nineteenth century[7].

Maran pledged all of his cultural allegiance to France, remarking during his early days in Ubangi–Shari:

> For now, with a French heart I feel that I am on the soil of my ancestors, ancestors of whom I disapprove because I have neither their primitive mentality nor their tastes, but they are ancestors nevertheless.[8]

Greater exposure to the local people appears to have strengthened his sense of racial solidarity, but never to have lessened his pride in his French assimilation.

Maran's strongest criticisms of colonialism occur in the preface rather than the novel itself, for his concern with objectivity precluded moralistic authorial intrusions. In the preface he emphasises the suffering, starvation and death that the authoritarian colonial administration and exploitative concession companies had brought to the people of Ubangi–Shari:

> The villages were decimated, the plantations disappeared, chickens and goats were annihilated. As for the natives, weakened by unceasing, excessive and unremunerated work, it was made impossible for them even to devote the necessary time to their sowing. They saw illness settle down among them, famine invade them and their number diminish.[9]

The conditions Maran described were so wide-spread in French Equatorial Africa that the population is estimated to have dropped from around 15,000,000 in 1900 to 2,860,686 in 1921.[10]

Although Maran hoped that *Batouala* would create a public awareness of maladministration in French Equatorial Africa, the fact finding commission sent to Ubangi–Shari in 1922 largely discredited his information. It was not until André Gide journeyed to this region in 1926 and published his *Voyage au Congo* (1927) that public pressure succeeded in bringing appreciable reform.

The novel, which takes place during the First World War, resolves around Batouala, a Banda chief, who becomes jealous when his favourite wife Yassigui'ndja takes an interest in Bissibi'ngui, a younger man. Angered by the advances and presumption of Bissibi'ngui, Batouala seeks his revenge by inviting the suitor to accompany him on a hunting expedition. However, fate undoes Batouala's plans, since the spear intended to murder Bissibi'ngui misses him and enrages a panther. Fatally mauled by the panther, Batouala dies in his hut a few weeks later, in the presence of Yassigui'ndja and Bissibi'ngui who think only of satisfying their passion.

In his portrayal of Batouala and Yassigui'ndja as well as Banda life, Maran has failed to explain local customs sufficiently to dispel the image of African 'primitiveness'. Even though he learned the Banda language, he appears to have used it more as a means of listening undetected to conversations among the Banda than as a tool for ethnographic research. In his private correspondence with Manoel Gahisto and Léon Bocquet, Maran reveals that he kept extensive notes on the 'curious things' he observed and read about, such as male and female circumcision, a 'copulation' dance and funeral rites, in order to make Batouala 'the reconstruction of the life of a Negro in general, and of a chief in particular'.[11]

In spite of Judith Gleason's contention that Maran has dignified Batouala, the author's treatment of him largely preserves the image of black self-indulgence, cruelty and credulity.[12] Although the chief has a total of nine wives, he satisfies his sexual appetites every morning with his favourite wife Yassigui'ndja:

> ... he wanted to fulfil his male desires, because, up to now, he has never missed doing so each morning before getting up for good. (p. 24)

Maran violates Banda tradition by making Yassigui'ndja Batouala's regular sexual partner for, according to Rev. Père Daigre, the Banda have strict rules governing a rotational system of cohabitation between a husband and each of his wives.[13] Not that polygamous husbands cannot have favourites among their wives, but they cannot show their preference by unequally lavishing their sexual favours. Thus, Maran depicts Batouala essentially as a monogamist—a jealous husband in a love triangle. The chief's self-indulgence also includes drunkenness which renders him grotesque:

> Meanwhile, more and more hideous, more and more drunk, Batouala got up to dance a few steps of the dance of love.
> He thought he was dancing, but he was only staggering, his head and legs heavy, his eyes red and swollen. He finally stumbled on a tree stump and sprawled at full length, laughing out a thick laugh. (p. 118)

Batouala's dog Djouma first introduces us to the cruelty of his master as well as that of the Banda tribe when he recollects his early days with his master. The chief trained the dog by beating it until blows and the fear of blows made it intelligent and obedient. The brutality the Bandas show towards their dogs—whipping, castrating and torturing them—becomes analogous to the treatment the whites give the Bandas:

> A dog is less than nothing. If they use him a little during the season of brush fire, it's because he knows how to flush out game

and excels in chasing it. Apart from that, since he is useless, they pay no attention to him except to thrash him. (p. 20)

Maran makes this comparison more apparent when Batouala tells his fellow tribesmen about white injustice and oppression:

>'We are only taxable flesh. We are only beasts of burden. Beasts? Not even that. Dogs? They feed them, and they care for their horses. Us? We are for them less than those animals; we are lower than the lowest. They are slowly crushing us.' (pp. 75–6)

During the 'dance of love' at the Ga'nza rites of passage, Batouala responds violently to Yassigui'ndja's and Bissibi'ngui's mutual desire. Seeing them fall to the ground as a couple, he foams with rage, hurls himself upon them with a knife, and vows as they escape unharmed:

>Ah! Those children of a dog even had the impudence to desire each other in front of him! He would have the skin of that whore, that child of a slut! As for Bissibi'ngui, he would castrate him! All the women would make fun of him then!
>The very audacity of it! Yassigui'ndja! To marry her hadn't he paid seven loincloths, a case of salt, three copper collars, a female dog, four cooking pots, thirty chickens, ten female goats, twenty-four large baskets full of millet, and a young slave!
>This accounting was right. He would make her go through the ordeals. (p. 88)

Batouala's instinctive reaction is one of murderous jealousy towards both his wife and her lover. His anger foreshadows his final act of walking from his deathbed to terrorise the couple in the midst of making love. The shift from oaths and threats to an inventory of the bride price he paid twelve years earlier, implies that he regards Yassigui'ndja primarily as property.

Later on when Batouala contemplates his revenge against Bissibi'ngui, he considers the panther method of murder as the most suitable:

>He is strangled. Afterwards, using a serrated knife, a cutting stone or iron claws, one slices the veins of the neck, as the panther

does, and, limb by limb, one dissects the victim, as the panther does. (p. 95)

Maran may be equating Batouala's cruelty with animality or using this type of assassination to reinforce the image of black 'savagery'.

Maran handles Batouala's extreme respect for tradition as an unthinking credulity rather than reasoned conservatism. The chief who questions and criticises white practices never directs his powers of inquiry and analysis towards his own culture. The author detracts from Batouala's stature by suggesting that he discerns little if any difference between personal habits and tribal traditions:

> Yawning and scratching are unimportant gestures. While continuing them, Batouala uttered a long series of grunts. That was a very old habit with him. It came to him from his parents. His parents had inherited it from theirs. The old customs are always the best. For the most part, they are founded on the surest experience. So one would never be able to follow them too closely.
>
> So thought Batouala. As a guardian of obsolete customs, he remained faithful to the traditions which his ancestors had passed on to him, but didn't go deeply into anything outside of that. If anything were in opposition to custom, all reasoning was useless. (p. 23)

The idea that the chief contemplates customs with seriousness appears somewhat ironical, since the author has made it clear that he follows without question whatever the ancestors did. Maran's opinion misrepresents Batouala, for he spends a great deal of time in the novel reflecting upon the differences between blacks and whites. Furthermore, the author does not permit the chief to live according to his belief that one can never follow customs too closely, because he shows him breaking the traditional regulations of polygamy and emphasises his procrastination in beating out the drum invitation for the Ga'nza celebration.

Batouala's dogmatic devotion to tribal customs serves as a foil to Bissibi'ngui's subordination of them to personal gratification and ambition. The young man gravitates towards other men's wives with no qualms about transgressing Banda laws against adultery. His attitude towards colonialism also counterbalances Batouala's, since he seeks to align himself with the whites as a militiaman:

'Thus, instead of paying taxes, it is we who help collect them. We do that by ransacking both the taxable villages and those who have paid their due. We have the rubber worked and recruit the men who are needed to carry the sandoukous.

'Such is the work of the militiamen. Chiefs and their men weigh him down with gifts to win his favor. Those little satisfactions make the tourougou's life sweet, pleasant, easy, indeed delightful, even more so because the commandants hardly know the language of the country they are administering . . .' (p. 108)

Batoula, on the other hand, has an uncompromising hatred for white men, swearing 'until my last breath, I will reproach them for their cruelty, their duplicity, their greed' (p. 75). Charles L. James views both Batouala and Bissibi'ngui as victims of colonialism, for white intrusion has made the former 'a living anachronism' bound to worn-out traditions and the latter a corrupt and rootless opportunist.[14] Thus, Batouala's death becomes symbolic, since the 'man with the lightning stick' has brought disintegration to Banda culture and doom to men who enshrine the past.

Maran's handling of Yassigui'ndja upholds the stock notion of black sensuality so completely that she builds her whole life around the pursuit of sexual pleasure. Finding daily relations with Batouala insufficient to quench her sexual passions, she lusts after Bissibi'ngui's virile body:

> In spite of her age she still felt young and rich in unused passion. The fire which devoured her could not be quenched by the one sexual experience her husband provided her each day. Why was it surprising that her virtue became more and more unstable every day? Batouala's stinginess was becoming quite insulting. Why didn't he try to raise himself to Bissibi'ngui's level? People were saying that Bissibi'ngui used to his heart's content that which makes a man know that he is a man. All the women doted on him—and so did she. (p. 45)

Although she considers Batouala a good husband, she places her sexual satisfaction above her loyalty to him. She sees no value in self-denial, because 'a woman should never refuse the desire of a man, especially when that man pleases her. That is a functional principle. The only law is instinct.' (p. 36).

In portraying Yassigui'ndja as a woman interested in sexuality only as an end in itself and not for procreation, Maran distorts her role as a Banda wife. He mentions her first pregnancy merely as a way of explaining the rationale behind polygamy, since Banda women must abstain from sexual relations while carrying and nursing a child. Even though her child died a few months after birth, he does not place any importance on Yassigui'ndja's childlessness after twelve years of marriage and ignores the tragedy of being childless in a culture that extols maternity. He consequently overplays the jealousy of Batouala's other wives towards Yassigui'ndja, for their maternity gives them a distinct social advantage over her as well as a deep-seated sense of superiority.

Maran's most vivid images of black 'savagery' lie in his discriptions of Banda life before colonialism and the orgiastic Ga'nza rite of passage. On these occasions he misrepresents Banda traditional life by lifting customs, especially those that shock European sensibilities, out of their cultural context. For example, he characterises Banda life prior to the white man's arrival as:

> Working little, and only for oneself, eating, drinking, and sleeping; at long intervals, some bloody ceremonies when they took out the livers of the dead in order to eat their courage and to absorb it—those were the only tasks of the blacks in other times, before the arrival of the whites. (p. 76)

This overgeneralisation sustains the European image of Africans as 'lazy, cannibalistic savages'. Maran undermines his explanation of the infrequency of the ritual of eating the livers of the dead by identifying it along with eating, drinking and sleeping as the only tasks of the men. By emphasising this ritual he seems to insure, despite his claims of 'objectivity', that it will impress the reader and play upon stock concepts of African 'primitiveness'.

The chapter on the Ga'nza remains one of the most memorable scenes of unbridled passion in French colonial literature. It also represents one of the greatest distortions of African culture, for Maran has fused male circumcision, female circumcision, and a ritualistic dance of love into a public orgy of drunkenness and sexuality. He appears to have combined many of the notes he referred to in his correspondence with Gahisto and Bocquet to form a potpourri of misinterpreted ethnographic material. At his Ga'nza young men and women, circumcised simultaneously in front of the whole tribe, begin dancing and singing after the operation, in spite of their pain and loss of blood. Although he does not describe the details of the male 'cutting', he graphically depicts female excision:

> The old woman summoned one of the dancers. Roughly separating her thighs, she seized with her fingers what had to be seized, stretching it like a rubber vine. With one blow—raou!—she cut; then, without even turning her head, threw the pieces of still warm and bloody flesh far into the crowd behind her.
> Why was so much importance attached to those pieces of flesh? As soon as they fell to the ground, the dogs angrily fought over them.(p. 85)

According to A. M. Vergiat, Banda male and female circumcision takes place separately on the bank of a local stream[15]. These events may not be witnessed by the general public and children as Maran states, but only by men who have been initiated in the case of the boys, and by male and female adult *ganzas* in the case of the girls. The excised flesh is discarded in the stream and the wound is immediately washed and dressed by the initiate's adult sponsor, i.e. a 'godfather' for a boy, a 'godmother' for a girl. After the operation and during the several weeks necessary for complete recovery, both internal and external medicines are given to the patient to promote rapid healing. In the evening, a number of hours after the operation, the boys dance to conquer their pain at their camp in the bush; the girls similarly dance in their communal lodging in the village. Therefore, Maran has not only neglected time intervals and telescoped various aspects of the Banda rites of passage into a single event, but has also substantially relied upon his own imagination. He has almost completely ignored the bush school which precedes circumcision, for the initiate must be fully steeped in his or her duties as a Banda man or woman before re-entering society as an adult. By following the initiation with a *danse de l'amour* and spontaneous love-making, Maran creates not a Banda Ga'nza but an African *Walpugisnacht*, celebrating nudity, sexuality and 'savagery'.

Nicolas Godian contends that Maran preserves stereotypes in *Batouala*, because his cultural assimilation made him 'too rationalist, too French to accept the Banda view of the world'[16]. Indeed, Maran shows less concern with Banda culture than with the colonial abuses that have caused local suffering; he is not trying to change the French image of the colonised so much as the French image of themselves as colonisers. Yet his novel never degenerates into a political polemic or loses its polished prose style. His sympathetic portraits of the African landscape endow the continent with a special dignity, countering Loti's hostile descriptions in *Roman d'un spahi*. Batouala becomes most noble when he pleads for the humane treatment of blacks and professes the brotherhood of all men shortly before his death. Maran's misrepresentation of Banda life unfortunately makes Batouala's seamy side the more memorable and turns his human weaknesses into 'African traits'. Nonetheless, Maran deserves his place in both French and African literary history, for as Lilyan Kestleloot has observed, he was 'the first black man in France to have dared to tell the truth about certain methods of colonisation and to have revealed ... what they [blacks] thought of European occupation'[17].

Gaston Adrien Joseph's novel *Koffi: roman vrai d'un noir* was intentionally written to 'correct' the images of French colonialists and Africans in *Batouala: véritable roman nègre*. Joseph, who joined the French Colonial Service in 1907, served in the Ivory Coast in increasingly responsible administrative positions until 1925 when he went to Paris as an official in the French Colonial Ministry. During his years in the Ivory Coast he published two nonfiction works about the country in addition to *Koffi*, which received the grand prix de littérature coloniale in 1923.

Koffi is a picaresque novel which traces the life of a servant Koffi from the age of nine until his death at about forty–three. Joseph, unwilling to accept Maran's negative definition of the French *mission civilisatrice* in the colonies, shows the benefits and refinements that Westernization brings Koffi. The author seems to suggest that the dilemma of people like Koffi arises from the African misunderstanding of French culture, which causes them to be too superficially French to be African and too basically African to be French.

In the novel Koffi, impressed by the Western clothes of Yao, a former village boy who now works for the whites, decides to join him in Aboisso. Under the tutelage of Yao, he learns about doing things in *la manière des blancs* and begins his career as a domestic servant. Starting as a kitchen helper, he later becomes a boy for a trader, a camping steward for an administrator, a cook, an interpreter and, finally, an elected tribal king. Although he attempts to rule his subjects progressively and bring them 'civilisation', the local priests resent his measures and instigate unrest. As the situation deteriorates so does Koffi, who little by little loses his semblance of

European assimilation and lapses into fetishism and alcoholism. Finally, Koffi's failure to supply requested porters and his inability to control his subjects prompts the French administration to sentence him to exile in Gabon, where he dies a few years later of alcoholism.

Koffi's esteem for Europeans diametrically opposes Batouala's avowed hatred of them until his declaration of brotherhood on his death–bed. Batouala comes closest to sharing some of Koffi's appreciation for Europeans when he thinks about white technology, for then his anger changes into a mixture of admiration and fear. However, Koffi's high regard for whites never wavers, since even during his exile 'he still held the same admiration for whites and their achievements that he had held when he worked for them'[18]. In a long passage which seems designed to refute Batouala's five–page denunciation of white worthlessness and colonial oppression, Koffi assures the people of his home village of the goodness of the whites:

> 'I have lived with the whites for a long time' said Koffi. 'I can assure you that they want only what is best for our welfare, nothing but our welfare. Carry out their orders, which are always prompted by common sense and are in your interest, even if you have not yet grasped their full significance. You formerly lived like animals and not like men. The whites are devoting themselves to the mission of improving your lot. Listen to their advice. Don't remain slaves to old prejudices, and don't stand in the way of their work. Let yourselves be guided by them. They know everything. You know nothing. My wish is that many of you will have the opportunity to visit our brothers in the south. You will then understand the favourable changes that the whites have brought to their área and which our region will profit from later on. The priests, the guides of our consciences, must be better informed of the blessings that our masters are obtaining for us, and you must send your children to school where they will come to know the benefits of white customs'.(pp. 177–8)

Besides preaching the gospel of colonial salvation, Koffi demonstrates the degree to which he has rejected the traditions of his parents and divorced himself from his roots. He extends his premise—that whites are superior to blacks—to himself, implying that his contact with Europeans makes him superior to the people of his village. Unlike Batouala, he looks upon the days prior to the arrival of the whites with disdain instead of nostalgia. He counters Batouala's charges that whites 'don't like us. They came to our land just to suppress us.' (*Batouala*, p. 74) with a portrait of white benevolence.

Koffi exemplifies black imitativeness, confusing the outer trappings of French culture with its fundamentals. From the time he leaves his village, being 'civilised' largely means wearing Western clothes no matter how ill-fitting. He treasures the old tattered kepi Yao gave him when he first arrived in Aboisso as a badge of his assimilation, even though 'it suited the urchin like gloves on a turtle, covering him from his eyebrows to the back of his head' (p. 36). After he learns to read, mail order catalogues from France become his favourite reading matter. Joseph perceives Koffi's fixation with Western dress as 'a weakness of blacks as soon as they have had even a little contact with civilisation' (p. 67).

The author especially ridicules Koffi's imitativeness when he founds a society for domestic servants, 'The Smart Set of Abidjan'. The Saturday night social meetings of this group conform to Koffi's definition of 'culture':

> Consequently, on Saturday night the members of the new group gathered together in a roomy wooden hut in the neighbourhood of Cocody. They were accompanied by their wives and friends who were odiously powdered and perfumed, dressed in their most beautiful *pagnes*, and coifed with multicoloured scarves. Although they tried to speak proper French, they used misunderstood words that they had heard in the kitchen or had gleaned by chance among the longest and most sonorous words in the dictionary. They danced in the manner of whites to the sound of an accordion which somehow or other managed to play *Viens Poupoule* and *La Madelon*. (p. 157)

What Koffi regards as the epitome of civilisation suggests bad taste at its very worst.

Throughout most of the novel, except for the few months when Koffi works for coarse and officious employers, he fulfills the stock role of the 'good servant'. Joseph characterises his devotion to M. Casanova who fosters his education and the administrator Léré who promotes him from cook to interpreter as 'the love of a Newfoundland dog' (p. 82). When M. Casanova, whom Koffi calls his 'father and mother' departs for France, he feels so orphaned and heartbroken that he loses his appetite. Later on he transfers these affections to M. Léré:

> The domestic servant of the Administrator had been hired this time as a cook. However, he would even have agreed to becoming a potwasher again in order to return to his home region and to serve his old master once more. (pp. 170–1)

His loyalty to his master is so great that he would gladly work for him in any capacity.

After Léré appoints Koffi to the administrative position of interpreter, the African expands his concept of devotion to his employer to include fidelity to the French administration. He works for the Colonial Government with the same enthusiasm he earlier displayed towards Casanova and Léré:

> Sworn in and the owner of a uniform, the former domestic filled his administrative post with a faithfulness and impartiality that rapidly earned him the respect of his subordinates and the increased esteem of his boss. (pp. 180–1).

Koffi moves from the 'good servant' to the 'good civil servant', executing all of his duties with conscientiousness. The author makes it evident in the novel that this transition is possible primarily because of the personal evolution Koffi has undergone during his years as a domestic.

Koffi as a local king, however, discovers that his Westernisation has not been complete enough to enable him to withstand the pressures of traditional life. Little by little he loses the high principles he upheld as an interpreter and when he suspects the offended local priests of casting spells on him, he visits a sorcerer at the suggestion of his wife. Thereafter, he places protective objects and statues around his home and begins wearing amulets to ward off evil, because 'his reversion was permanent. Koffi was at the mercy of the cults of his tribe' (p. 202). Frustrated in all of his endeavours to introduce 'civilisation', he succumbs to lassitude and alcoholism. Joseph mentions Koffi's age several times during this section of the novel, emphasising the irony that a few years back in the tribe totally efface the traces of twenty years spent with Europeans.

In addition to the stereotypes Joseph preserves in his portrayal of Koffi, he reinforces those of black childishness, 'primitiveness' and laziness in his treatment of Africans in general. Although he never explicitly calls Africans children, he draws an extended analogy between a school master training 'the minds of his children' and the French administrator trying to bring advancement to the 'natives' (p. 212). When the administrator M. Léré discovers two calabashes full of palmnuts and fruit placed in front of his phonograph, he listens to his boy with good-humoured paternalism:

> 'It's him, commandant. He says the folks of Kanango were very happy to listen to your phonograph last night. Therefore, they told this kid to put that near the box in order to feed the little white man who is inside. And so, the 'bushmen' believe the little white man in there is going to make music again today.' (pp. 107–8)

Léré, charmed by this unforeseen explanation, registers his pleasure by giving the little boy two coins, then dismisses the incident as a quaint example of African naïveté. (Actually, the presentation of gifts to the phonograph constitutes a logical extension of animism and its concept of votive offerings.)

In one of the longest digressions in Koffi, Joseph equates African 'primitivism' with a lack of aesthetic appreciation. He claims that Africans have no sense of artistic taste, 'for nothing is ugly in the eyes of the primitive . . . no artistic feeling moves these retarded peoples of the planet' (p. 113). Contending that beauty for the 'savage' in the forest regions of tropical Africa is only fecundity, he devalues African art forms in this manner:

> Perhaps in the dance one should be able to find a feeble sign of art? But no, with its gestures and lascivious contortions, it is in reality a parody of the act of procreation. (p. 113)

The author most approximates Maran's depiction of sensuality and bestiality when he describes the frenzied dance of a fetish priestess and the rites of Koffi's coronation. Even though he fails to conjure the powerful images of Maran, he summarises and judges these events as examples of savagery which illustrate 'the characteristic stamp of the primitive mentality of these human beings, these people's fundamental barbarism, simmering with brutal sensations' (p. 117).

He presents laziness as the primary African trait that impedes the development of the colonies. In an apparent projection of his own opinions onto Koffi, he recounts the newly-crowned king's struggle against the idleness of his people:

> The young chief of his tribe struggled wholeheartedly against the inertia and laziness of his people whom he wished to emancipate—to draw out of a kind of lethargy that was letting them vegetate in habit, barbarism, and destitution.(p. 213)

Joseph implies that the transformation of African lethargy into industry will fairly automatically end African 'barbarism' and poverty.

In spite of Koffi's failures as a *pseudo-assimilé*, the author does not use him to negate the value of French colonialism and *la mission civilisatrice*. Koffi's problems emanate not from having watched and imitated whites, but from not having been sufficiently educated to observe them with understanding. Since Joseph's thesis is that colonialism is noble, he invokes a number of stereotypes that reinforce the dependency of Africans and demonstrate the necessity of colonialism. In the final analysis, Koffi stands not only as Gaston Joseph's personal refutation of *Batouala*, but also as that of the French Colonial Service.

The fact that the authors in this chapter have perpetuated many of the same stereotypes of Africans has not really made their novels homogeneous. The role which these images play varies according to the message of each author. Southon and Joseph show the greatest affinity, for each of them is using African inferiority to justify either missionary or colonial endeavour. Maran's dependence on stock 'African traits' seems to suggest a psychological need to distance himself from the Africans who offended his French cultural sensibilities. Greene appears to have chosen and exploited the 'good servant' for primarily artistic and religious reasons, since Ali's trust and obedience not only make him a foil to Scobie but also serve as virtues within the framework of Catholicism.

NOTES

1. Arthur Eustace Southon, *A Yellow Napoleon: A Romance of West Africa* (Freeport, New York: Books for Libraries Press, 1972; first published in 1928) p. 14. All subsequent page references will be to this edition and will follow immediately in the text.

2. G. D. Killam, *Africa in English Fiction 1874–1939* (Ibadan: Ibadan Univ. Press, 1968) p. 54.
3. Graham Greene, *The Heart of the Matter* (New York: Viking Press, 1971) p. 16. All subsequent page references will be to this edition and will follow immediately in the text.
4. Derek Traversi, 'Graham Greene: II. The Later Novels', *The Twentieth Century*, vol. cxlix, no. 890 (April 1951) p. 325.
5. Traversi, p. 324. Kai Laitinen, 'The Heart of the Novel: The Turning Point in *The Heart of the Matter*', in *Graham Greene: Some Critical Considerations*, ed. by Robert O. Evans (Lexington: Univ. of Kentucky Press, 1963) p. 171.
6. Mercer Cook, *Five French Negro Authors* (Washington, D.C.: The Associated Publishers, Inc., 1943) p. 131.
7. Léopold Sédar Senghor, 'René Maran, précurseur de la Négritude', in *Hommage à René Maran* (Paris: Présence Africaine, 1965) pp. 9 and 13. Trans. is mine.
8. Cook, p. 130.
9. René Maran, *Batouala: A True Black Novel*, trans. by Barbara Beck and Alexandre Mboukou (London: Heinemann Educational Books, 1973) p. 12. All subsequent page references will be to this edition and will follow immediately in the text.
10. Jean Suret-Canale, *French Colonialism in Tropical Africa 1900–1945*, trans. by Till Gottheiner (New York: Pica Press, 1971) p. 36. Much of this decline has been attributed to the administration's misuse of the *Indigénat* code, forced labour and taxation to require Africans to gather rubber and engaged in porterage. Since the concession companies enjoyed a complete monopoly and greatly underpaid the local people for the rubber they collected, Cohen observes that in 1919 natives in the Congo had to work 60 to 120 days a year to earn the eight francs for their annual personal tax. Persons who failed to meet either government or company demands suffered harsh reprisals, including severe corporal punishment, the destruction of personal property, and the abduction of wives and children. See Cohen, *Rulers of Empire*, pp. 70–1, 78–81.
11. Manoel Gahisto, 'Le Genèse de *Batouala*', in *Hommage à René Maran*, p. 131. Trans. is mine.
12. Judith Illsley Gleason, *This Africa: Novels by West Africans in English and French* (Evanston, Ill.: Northwestern Univ. Press, 1965) p. 75.
13. Rev. Père Daigre, C. S. Sp., 'Les Bandas de l'Oubangui–Chari (Afrique Equatoriale Française)', *Anthropos*, vol. 26 (1931) p. 663.
14. Charles L. James, '*Batouala*: René Maran and the Art of Objectivity', *Studies in Black Literature*, vol. iv, no. 3 (Autumn 1973) pp. 21–2.
15. A. M. Vergiat, *Les Rites secrets des primitifs de l'Oubangui* (Paris: Payot, 1951) pp. 76–8, 92–4.
16. Nicolas Godian, '*Batouala* Reassessed', *West Africa*, no. 2934 (3 Sept. 1973) p. 1230.
17. Lilyan Kestleloot, 'René Maran and *Batouala*', *Pan-African Journal*, vol. v, no. 1 (Spring 1972) p. 55.
18. Gaston Joseph, *Koffi: roman vrai d'un noir* (Paris: Editions du Monde Nouveau, 1922) p. 228. All subsequent page references will be to this edition and will follow immediately in the text. All translations of *Koffi* are mine.

4 Stereotypes Contradicted: *The Leopard Priestess* and *Toum*

Novels expressly written in reaction against stereotypes frequently include a number of digressions which specifically refute major misconceptions about Africans. In addition their characters often display only those traits that counteract the pejorative ones popularly associated with Africans. In their most extreme form these works merely substitute positive caricatures of Africans for the more familiar negative ones.

The Leopard Priestess (1934) by Robert S. Rattray and *Toum* (1926) by Robert Delavignette remain two of the finest examples in British and French colonial literature of novels which deliberately contradict stereotypes.

Captain Robert Sutherland Rattray, who joined the British Colonial Civil Service in 1907, spent over twenty-five years in Ghana. After establishing the Anthropology Department of the Gold Coast Government in 1921, he devoted most of the rest of his life to gathering field data for his scholarly publications on Ashanti law, religion, art, and folklore. His only novel, set in pre-colonial Ashanti–land, remains one of the most successful British depictions of Africans and African life. While he has not allowed anthropology to eclipse his artistic concerns, he does use it to educate the reader, as he explains in his introduction to the novel:

> The story has been written as a novel but the main facts and also most of the dialogue are as I heard them from my native friends. I have endeavoured to make my characters speak, act, and react, as unsophisticated Africans would. Of what is about to be recorded some part might possibly be classified as Anthropology. Although I hasten to disclaim any such dull intention, I have hopes that the tale may serve a purpose,

because, some times with little real knowledge of Africa's past history, traditions, legal code, constitution, religion, we have attempted to build up working plans of Government for various regions, which are ostensibly based on native institutions but in reality are sometimes only our own Western ideas of constitutional Government under a thin disguise.[1]

The novel centres around the forbidden love of two members of the Leopard Clan—Opoku, a young hunter, and Amalagane, the adolescent priestess of the arrow poison. Although there is no consanguinity, by tribal law they are siblings and their love is incestuous. Until Opoku becomes initiated, he worries only about Amalagane's violation of her vow of chastity being discovered by the 'cutter' during the rite of female circumcision. Thereafter, he understands that their transgression could cause the infertility of the land and the clan, and the impotence of the arrow poison. A sense of foreboding develops and the elders resolve to let the excision ceremony justify or dispel their fears about Amalagane. Opoku, who has bribed the 'cutter' so that he will declare her a virgin, goes on an elephant hunt to test the power of the arrow poison but fails to return. Soon after the excision Amalagane marries a member of the nearby Porcupine Clan and bears him Opoku's son. When Opoku finally returns, he unsuccessfully begs her to leave her husband and flee with him. After she is killed by a black mamba, he carries her corpse into the forest and confesses his sin to his father before thrusting a poison arrow into his hip. A fire then consumes the grove where the dead lovers lie, and a pair of leopards emerge from the flames.

In *The Leopard Priestess* Rattray concentrates on both the inner and outer lives of his main characters, drawing Opoku and Amalagane with distinctly different personalities. Opoku, the more conservative of the two, does not question tribal traditions and customs until the end of the novel. His response to his father's teachings during his initiation is one of guilt:

> Opoku had sat unhappy and uneasy throughout this lengthy dissertation. Every detail of his illicit relationship with his 'sister' had risen vividly before his mind's eye. Those parts of his father's narrative which had a bearing on this had overshadowed, almost obliterated all the rest. Most of it, indeed, he had only been vaguely aware of, as one is aware of a background in a scene

where some dreadful drama is being enacted at the forefront of the stage. He was not so much torn between his infatuation of Amalagane and the terrible consequences which he now knew would follow if he persisted in indulging it, as distracted to know how he could prevent what had already happened from becoming known, and how, if that were possible, he could ward off what seemed the inevitable consequences of what they had done. The future only held danger because of the past. There would never be a repetition of that mad folly. His father had spoken of expiation of sin. Was there then a way out? Suicide, murder, flight, each in turn flashed across his mind. (p. 73)

Opoku experiences a deep sense of desperation, for he now knows that his sin constitutes a failure to meet his moral obligation for the welfare of the clan.

During her initiation, Amalagane, whose nature is that of a revolutionary, objects to this taboo as a violation of her personal freedom:

> She, as he [Opoku] had been, was intent only on the law which forbade all thought of marriage between them—the law which they had already secretly transgressed. But the feelings which her instructress's lesson roused in her were far unlike his. Her whole being, as she sat and listened, rebelled against these man–made rules and prohibitions. She was a lovely young animal, who demanded the right to select her own mate and, having made the selection, to keep what she had won. (p. 78)

Amalagane remains the more individualistic and assertive of the two throughout most of the novel. Before the 'cutting' she tries to persuade Opoku to run away from the clan with her, but he voices objections based on the traditions of clan life. In answer to his question about what will happen to their ancestral spirits if they flee, she boldly replies:

> 'We will leave them behind, only taking a little earth from your ancestor's shrine and mine, and where we settle we will build a new shrine and your sons will sacrifice upon it.' (p. 165)

Only at the end of the novel is Opoku willing to escape with her, but by then their roles have reversed and she has lost her rebellious spirit.

In his treatment of Amalagane, Rattray has broken the literary image of the African woman as merely a sex object or a drudge. He presents her as a believable character of passion, intelligence, and will. He prevents her conservatism at the end of the story from confirming stereotypes of female subservience by ascribing it to her increased maturity, maternal responsibilities, and perhaps a 'subtle psychological change due to mutilation'. (p. 208)

In the long chapter in which Opoku stalks a swamp elephant, Rattray portrays the hunter as deeply sensitive to nature, intelligent and reflective. In searching for the elephant, he is also seeking within himself for an understanding of Amalagane's love for him and his for her:

> A woman's desire, he thought, must be a wonderful thing to inspire her to take risks concerning which his own stout heart had still misgivings, to make her willing to give up associations which had always seemed to him to be part of their lives, to cause her to rebel against laws which he had thought inviolate and inviolable. Flight! Why was it, he wondered, that he had not thought of this way out of their difficulties himself? Of course, it was because he had hitherto considered the results of his actions not in terms of himself but of his family, his clan, his tribe. How simple things would be if one had only one's self to consider! (p. 173)

This passage demonstrates a major attitudinal change, for it shows Opoku beginning to elevate his allegiance to Amalagane above that to the clan.

Rattray uses the rest of Opoku's hunting trip to dispel the stereotypes of black faithlessness and cowardice, for after killing the elephant, he tries desperately to keep his promise to Amalagane that he will return before the 'cutting'. Battling a flooded plain and swamp, he reaches his first camp site just as the drums tell of Amalagane's virginity. At that moment the parallel between his objective and subjective quests is complete; having first affirmed the strength of the arrow poison, he now affirms the strength of his love for her. This love sustains him during his months of fever and malnutrition in the forest, for when he finally returns, he calls, 'Where is my wife?' before he faints from weakness (p. 196). Although Rattray handles this event with extreme economy, he presents the hunter's survival as a triumph of the tenacious spirit of man.

Occasionally the author interrupts the flow of narrative with long explanations of ceremonies which are about to occur. Many of these passages expressly refute European prejudices, as shown by these comments about divination:

> It would not be just to dismiss all this as chicanery. It is the African's way of seeking an unbiased answer for his doubts and questioning, and thus, to ease his mind. It enables him, also, to place the onus of certain unpleasant but wholesome truths on the shoulders of the spirits and to fix in the same quarter the opprobium of carrying out unpopular but salutary measures.
>
> It is equally good psychology and policy, because in nine cases out of ten the soothsayer's wand will bend to the trend of public opinion. (pp. 107-8)

Rattray acquaints the reader with the fundamentals of traditional Ashanti law and government by clarifying the position of the Master of the Earth and illustrating his method of dealing with the elders of the Leopard Clan:

> This was the Master of the Earth, the Priest–King of this African tribe. Yet although he might be described as 'Chief' or 'King', his position was quite unlike that which these titles convey to the European mind. No binding law of primogeniture governed his election. He was chosen by a group of Elders from among the direct descendants of the senior remote ancestor from whom all ultimately claimed descent. (p. 120)
>
> ... The Master of the Earth spoke not as if he was prosecutor or counsel for defence, but rather as a wise judge who directs and guides a jury whose task it is to give the verdict. (p. 124)

In pointing to the Master of the Earth as an elected official accessible to his constituents, Rattray negates the popular conception of tribal rulers as dictators. He later addresses himself to the stereotype of African laziness, showing that work so dominates traditional village life that even children's games are functional:

> ... she [Amalagane] was returning from the forest carrying a bundle of firewood, accompanied by some little girls, scarcely

more than infants, each staggering under her small load of faggots; for the African child's only toys and games consist in playing at the work upon which their elders are so incessantly engaged. In this manner they not only assist the grown-ups but also unconsciously learn to fit themselves for household duties. (pp. 129-30)

Through his characterisation of Opoku and Amalagane as well as his authorial intrusions, Rattray projects an image of Africans as intelligent, hardworking, and respectable. Their high regard for their culture and traditions becomes a strength rather than an enslavement, for he deeply admires the cohesiveness of African village and family life. Yet in writing *The Leopard Priestess*, Rattray has done more than dispel old stereotypes and affirm the dignity of Africans. He has created a polished work of fiction and handled characterisation, description, and dialogue with literary sensibilities. As a British depiction of African traditional life, it merits Killam's praise as 'quite the most remarkable novel devoted to this theme produced during this period [1900-39]—one might almost say to date'.[2]

Robert Louis Delavignette attempts in *Toum* to present both the colonised and the coloniser from the point of view of each other as well as themselves. Delavignette, who entered the colonial administration in 1919 as an agent of civil affairs, was appointed to the Corps of Colonial Administrators in 1922, spending two years in Niger and four in Upper Volta. By the time illness and fatigue forced him to leave Africa his reputation for effective leadership was so widely recognised that Governor-General Jules Carde praised him as 'the best administrator of his generation'.[3] By approaching Africans with openmindedness and respect, Delavignette successfully combined the administrative goals of increasing agricultural production and tax revenues with his humanitarian one of improving the local standard of living.

The novel *Toum*, published under the pseudonym Louis Faivre, represents Delavignette's earliest effort to make French colonial administrators aware of the humanity of Africans. This work, set in Niger during the early 1920s, is largely conceived as an image study that reveals African and European perceptions of each other.

The plot centres around the relationship between a young French administrator, simply called Monsieur, and Toum, the village girl he takes as his 'bush wife'. The African narrator of the story supplies the following summary:

> I am telling the true story of a man and a woman: a slave girl from a poor village and a white man, newer to our country than anyone else.
> He found her in the bush. She shared his bed. At first he believed she was a pet animal and played with her. By the time he realized that she was a woman, she already knew that he was only a man.[4]

Yet, this synopsis somewhat misrepresents the book, since the novelist places greater emphasis on local customs and the way Nigériens view the French than on the way Monsieur changes his image of Toum. Like Rudbeck in Joyce Cary's *Mister Johnson*, Monsieur achieves an understanding of Toum as a person only at the end of the novel. The factors that influence his new perception of her appear to be her pregnancy, the death of their infant son shortly after birth, and a long conversation with three commandants about racial and colonial attitudes. Toum, on the other hand, always considers Monsieur a man, albeit a strange one, whose manners and culture differ too greatly from her own ever to foster her emotional happiness. Her joys in the novel come not from her husband, but her activities and conversations with the local people of Yataoua.

At the beginning of the novel, Toum and her mother Dela, forced to flee from the village Seminaire de Cavaliers as victims of ethnic prejudice, encounter the Frenchman who tells them to go to the French Court at Yataoua. When they arrive, the Sultan of the city decides to confiscate the young girl, but Monsieur secures her release and takes her as his 'native' wife. The mother then goes back to the village where the prestige of having a daughter who lives with a white man assures her social acceptance. Toum's life changes from one of deprivation to one of ease, for the Frenchman's money enables her to enjoy the luxuries of her own culture. Monsieur gives her the name 'Toum', a shortened form of the local word *toumtia* (ewe), since her 'high-pitched voice, profile with a snub-nose, and gentle soul' remind him of a sheep (p. 97). Limited by age, language and cultural barriers, their relationship remains at the physical and habitual level until Monsieur appreciates her as an individual. After his death from a tropical fever, Toum returns to her village as a well-fed and wealthy woman.

African Stereotypes Contradicted

What gives momentum to the novel is the basic tension between the narrator's and Monsieur's images of the same Nigériens. Essentially, this technique dispels stereotypes through comparison and contrast, measuring the fullness of Nigérien characters against the narrowness of European racist clichés. Much of this process occurs in the mind of the reader, for the narrator usually refrains from commenting upon these differences, reserving his intrusions for general discussions of African philosophy. Although the author presents all of his Nigériens as people instead of types, he especially breaks the stereotypes that Africans lack both love and intelligence in his handling of Dela, Toum's mother.

Dela, a slave woman, is ennobled by her sufferings as an 'outsider' in the village and her deep love for her daughter. Dela flees with her daughter when she is falsely accused of having caused the death of the chief's son after the latter killed her husband. When the Sultan of Yataoua promises protection in exchange for her daughter, Dela clings to Toum so tightly that guards must come to carry the girl away. Furthermore, despite her abject poverty, she gives the eunuch in charge of the harem all of the money the Sultan has just paid her as a bride price, in order to see Toum for 'a single second' (p. 59). The agony of being separated from her child by the Sultan emboldens her to plead her case before the Frenchman; later her desire to do what is best for Toum persuades her to let Monsieur 'marry' the girl. After she visits her daughter in the white man's house and sees that she is well-cared for, she parts from her with great feeling and solemnity:

> The moment for good-byes has come and Dela wants to leave in order to be on her way before dark; she will sleep in the next village at the home of some people Magagi told her about. She tells Fatima not to accompany her a little way as is customary.
>
> Mother and daughter hold hands. A look, a silence reunites them. For the first time, they are going to be separated. It's over. The old woman walks away. (p. 85)

The fact that Dela convinces her daughter not to accompany her seems to arise from her understanding that this marriage 'is not an ordinary marriage' (p. 83). Since Fatima (Toum) is now living in special conditions that fall outside of their traditions, her mother may see no reason for her to be bound by an old custom, or she may merely wish not to prolong the pain of saying good-bye. The dignity and silence of this voluntary farewell are impressive in their expression of so much tenderness and love.

Dela as a character is an exception to the 'unthinking' African, for she reflects upon both the past and the present, and anticipates the future. Even though she has succeeded in putting the events that happened to them in the village in mental perspective, she finds it more difficult to evaluate those that have occurred in the city:

> She looks at her daughter who has become the wife of a White man. How did this happen? A short time ago she fled through the countryside and thrust herself outside of the reach of traditional law. Yesterday she even resisted the will of the Sultan and today she is leaving her daughter to a White man!
>
> Life is too much for poor folks. If they escape one trap, they fall into another. If they don't want to roam around among the dangers of the bush and the night, they have to resign themselves to servitude.
>
> This White man isn't bad, Magagi told her. The child won't suffer. When Monsieur leaves, she'll come back to the village, rich and plump. In the end this marriage can't be judged by ordinary standards. Everything that deals with Whites is an exception to the rule. Don't they take a man as a prisoner or servant or soldier, a woman for a wife? You have to give in; it'll only be bad for a while. (pp. 83-4)

In spite of her fatalism in this passage, Dela's escape from the village, her appeal to the white man, and her permission for the marriage are all acts of decision and conscious will. As a result of her conversations with Magagi, she knows that she has changed not only her daughter's destiny but also her own, since Fatima will enjoy a few years of luxury and she will appease the offended chief of her village with the bride price she has received. A bit of the immunity that whites have from the traditional as well as the colonial rules will now extend to both her daughter and herself, transforming them from village outcasts into notables. While she philosophises that one must submit to what life brings, her intelligence and shrewdness have enabled her to select its best offerings.

In his portrayal of Toum, Delavignette breaks the literary image of the black woman as a sex object by showing the gap between her true personality and the one Monsieur ascribes to her. Convinced throughout most of the novel that she is a pet animal, he has no idea that she merely obeys and tolerates him, having found little in his culture and life style to admire. Far from considering the whites as 'civilised', she contends that 'the life of White men is something abnormal' (p. 112). Unlike Pierre Loti's deceitful Fatou–gaye, Toum makes no attempt to control her husband sexually or to take his money dishonestly. Instead, she regards herself as obliged to stay with him because of the bride price paid her mother, finding the wealth and ease of her new situation adequate compensations for her unsatisfying marriage.

Although Toum rarely shows her true emotions to her husband because 'a ewe has a great reputation for gentleness' (p. 98) his decision that she should go to school and learn French elicits her anger:

> Just think the wife of the administrator, someone who's going to be a mother, becoming the prisoner of a Dahomean all morning and afternoon! This eater of maize would beat her like he beats all of his pupils with sharp whacks of his ruler and would make her repeat awful nonsense.
>
> Good-bye to the good times at the guard camp, the idleness, the walks first thing in the morning that led her from street to street and from compound to compound. Good-bye to the heart to heart talks that would never be replaced by conversations with this White man. She wouldn't receive the latest news any more, she'd no longer take part in palavers and story–telling. What bad luck! Under the Dahomean's threats she'd be bleating out a nonsense language. (p. 205)

This passage reveals both her pride and her xenophobia. Her husband's plan offends her deeply, since it compromises her dignity and status as the wife of a white man. The fact that the schoolmaster is a Dahomean merely compounds her sense of injury, for she considers him her inferior. The term 'eater of maize' functions as an ethnic slur because the main staple of her diet is millet. She basically fears the brutality of the teacher and the disruption that Westernisation will bring to her life. Monsieur's docile ewe ironically denounces his language as senseless bleating. Far from being a thoughtless sex object, Toum is a person of strong will and intelligence who has no desire to become an *assimilée*.

Delavignette contradicts the popular idea of African ignorance by pointing out that it is mainly the French *corvée* (forced labour) instead of backwardness that keeps peasants from taking proper care of themselves. Road construction projects, for instance, require intensive labour during a crucial period for crop cultivation. Consequently, the threat of imprisonment or fines coerces men into jeopardising their food supply to bring 'modern progress':

> Under the escort of the horsemen and the guards, we gather at the spot where the white man wants his road. For eight, ten, twelve days we carry earth and water and our children pack the strip of wet earth, beating it rhythmically with little sticks. Bent over in a line, they go tap, tap, tap all day long, moving ahead step by step. And behind their tedious suffering the wide and hard road is born. Truly! For materials, the particles of our red earth, the precious water from our wells. For tools, our baskets, our earthenware jars, our hoes, our picks, our little sticks, our heads that carry, our hands that scratch and gather. For workers, ourselves. Those are the ingredients of the road in the language of the White man. And on this work that we redo every year during the rainy season when the fields beg for us, the White men bring out their marvellous machine. (pp. 141–2)

The narrator depicts the work as a costly intrusion upon the traditional patterns of village life that obligates local farmers to expend energy, waste water, and neglect their fields. The problem is European, not African, ignorance, for the coloniser remains unaware of the needs of the colonised.

A group of subsistence farmers are insulted by Monsieur when he glibly tells them that they must work harder. Filled with righteous indignation, they recount some of the special efforts they make to provide food for their families:

> 'Sometimes we go as far as two days' distance from the village to make our farms. Do you doubt that we don't do our utmost? We often sow twice only to harvest once, because the first sowing perished from the whim of the rains. What? Are we supposed to be masters of the earth and the sky?'. (p. 165)

Painfully aware of the poor soil and irregular rains that plague them, they do everything in their power to insure successful crops. Their hardships can be attributed to the difficult growing conditions in the Sahel and inadequate agricultural technology, but not to an unwillingness to work.

Even though Delavignette has a tendency to lose his focus in *Toum*, the novel is one of the most interesting French literary attempts to look at colonialism through African eyes.

Both Rattray and Delavignette are basically didactic writers, for each of them is endeavouring to reshape his readers' images of Africans. However, they go about this goal differently, since Rattray uses characterisation and occasional anthropological digression to correct stereotypes while Delavignette does so through multiple points of view. Of the two novels, *Toum* remains the more subtle, because Delavignette challenges misconceptions about Africans not so much by telling as by asking his readers to weigh his Nigérien characters against the distorted images his French characters have of them.

NOTES

1. Robert Sutherland Rattray, *The Leopard Priestess* (New York: D. Appleton-Century Comp., 1935; first published, 1934) p. 17. All subsequent page references will be to this edition and will follow immediately in the text.
2. Killam, *Africa*, p. 66.
3. Cohen, *Rulers of Empire*, p. 100.
4. Louis Faivre, pseud. of Robert Louis Delavignette, *Toum* (Paris: Bernard Grasset, 1926) p. 7. All subsequent page references will be to this edition, and will follow immediately in the text. This translation and all subsequent ones are mine.

5 Stereotypes Transcended: *Mister Johnson* and *Va-t'en avec les tiens*!

Only novels which present Africans as individuals rather than representatives of their race truly move beyond stereotypes. Since these works revolve almost exclusively around the unique personalities of their major African characters, their authors tend to be professional writers with a special talent for characterisation. Joyce Cary and Christine Garnier, in centring their novels *Mister Johnson* (1931) and *Va-t'en avec les tiens*! (1951) on an exuberant office clerk and an introspective maternity nurse, have created not only two of the most deeply human but also two of the most memorable characters in British and French colonial literature.

Joyce Cary served as a District Officer in the British Colonial Service in Northern Nigeria from 1913 until 1920 when ill health forced him to retire. He once described his duties during his first tour in the field as follows:

> As an acting district officer, in almost the humblest rank of the service, I was in charge of two Emirates, stretching over a region bigger than Wales. There was no telegraph. A letter to Provincial H.Q. took three days or a week, according to the state of the roads and the Niger floods. I could not expect an answer in less than a week. My orders were to do what I thought necessary and take the consequences if I did wrong.[1]

Some of these early experiences as well as later ones from his road building days as the D.O. at Borgu have filtered after years of mature introspection into the substance of *Mister Johnson*.

In the novel Johnson displays some of the traits of the partially Westernized 'native' and 'good servant' in his imitativeness, lying, robbery and devotion to Rudbeck. However, he does not remain at

African Stereotypes Transcended 79

this stereotypical level even if he does so in the minds of Arnold Kettle and Frederick Karl.[2] Neither does he truly validate Killam's more subtle theory that he operates both as a person and a stereotype:

> There is a dichotomy in the characterisation of Johnson which we as readers respond to in two quite separate ways. Put simply, we either laugh with Johnson or we laugh at him. And this implies two quite separate systems of judgement. When we laugh with Johnson we share his joy and understand his irrepressible good spirits, his incredible self-reliance...
>
> But when we laugh at Johnson a different set of values, predicating different judgements, come into play. We look at him, like all of the Europeans in the novel, from the outside and determine that his way is different from ours, that our way is better because we would not make his mistakes. In these parts of the book Johnson is little more than the semi–literates caricatured by Hyne or decried by Bindloss.[3]

Killam confuses the reader's response with the author's technique in this passage. What he calls 'a dichotomy of characterisation' is really a dichotomy of *interpretation* on the part of the reader. If Johnson is seen as little more than a caricature of a semi-literate African in certain sections of the novel, Cary has been misread. He develops Johnson as a highly idiosyncratic individual who does everything in a uniquely 'Johnsonian' style. Even though the clerk has some of the characteristics associated with African stereotypes, Cary insures that he possesses them simply as an individual who happens to be African. He never presents Johnson as a generalised depiction of all partially Westernized Africans; Mister Johnson is just himself.

What critics overlook when they discuss Johnson's imitativeness is his power to bring Western objects into harmony with African tradition. For example, as the headman of all the road gangs, he exhibits his canopy chair and helmet as the emblem of his office like an African ruler or priest. These objects have lost their Western function and have become ceremonial pieces in an African sense, forming part of Johnson's ritual in visiting the gangs:

> He also buys himself a new canopy chair, a white helmet and a pair of patent–leather shoes. He wears the shoes on Sunday; on

the other days he goes barefoot, followed by a small boy, carrying the hat and the chair. Whenever he visits a gang, it is set up and the hat laid on the canopy, like a royal crown above the chair of state. Johnson himself, having thus displayed the marks of his rank, goes among the gang, to swap jokes with the drummers or improvise a chorus.[4]

For Johnson, straddling two different cultures does not necessarily mean elevating one at the expense of the other; often it involves blending some of their elements. In this instance, Johnson is not culturally incongruous but syncretic.

Throughout the novel, imagination rather than deception causes Johnson to embellish the truth. When Ajali, the clerk in Sergeant Gollup's store, accuses Johnson of lying about his conversation with Tring, the new Assistant District Officer, Cary explains:

> Johnson is angry because he feels that his description is even more truthful than Tring's bare words; that his speech, repeated in cold blood, could not possibly convey to a third party, certainly not to a stupid and suspicious person like Ajali, the real effect of this remarkable experience which still makes Johnson's heart beat with pride and gratitude. (p. 112)

Johnson, then, engages in exaggeration in order to communicate the truth of his subjective experience. It is not a question of being unable to discriminate between facts and feelings, but rather one of perceiving the latter as more significant.

Even when Rudbeck dismisses him for embezzlement—an act the officer himself has committed under the name of 'reappropriation'—Johnson maintains that he has never lied to or deceived his superior. To Johnson no fraud has occurred because he has thoroughly recorded all of the illegal funds spent on enticing 'pagans' to join the road work. His beer cash book and his forgetfulness in personal money matters exonerate him in his own mind:

> He [Johnson] has never troubled himself about money; he has much more interesting things to think about. But he knows very well that he has given all his devotion to Rudbeck and that what he may have spent on some trifling necessities for himself is nothing to what he has paid out for Rudbeck's road. (pp. 191–2)

Essentially the ends justify the means for both Johnson and Rudbeck, but Johnson, unaware of how far the rules may safely be manipulated, stands outside of the aegis of the colonial bureaucracy. Similarly Johnson's small robberies of Gollup's cash box do not confirm the stereotype of Africans as thieves. According to Sheka Hassan Kanu, Johnson has equated Western culture with cash values so completely that prodigality certifies his 'civilisation'.[5] Practically all of the money he takes from Gollup, however, pays for local beer and drummers at his parties instead of Western goods. It is money which enables him, as an outsider from the South, to break down the resistance of the people of Fada to himself and his ideas. Bamu's family pays no attention to his marriage proposal until he offers a high bride price; the chiefs will not send men to the road gangs until he tells them about cash prizes. Whatever access he has to Western and traditional culture largely comes from having money, because both systems willingly exploit his extravagance.

The devotion Johnson shows towards Rudbeck far exceeds the slavish obedience of the 'good servant'. Johnson considers Rudbeck his friend and dedicates all of his energies to realising the officer's dream of road building. In a reversal of the usual pattern, Johnson imaginatively inspires Rudbeck and becomes the creative genius behind the Fada road. On one occasion the Britisher even publicly acknowledges the relationship between Johnson and himself by introducing him to the Resident Bulteel as 'the man with the ideas' (p. 162).

If Cary rises above the stereotypes of African imitativeness, lying, robbery and devotion in portraying Mister Johnson, how does he characterise the young clerk? First of all, he points to him as a creative, imaginative artist infused with a positive life force. Not only does Cary repeatedly refer to him as a 'poet' and 'artist', but he also continually shows him in the process of creating, improvising, and inventing. Johnson is an alchemist who transmutes everything he absorbs into artistic self-expression:

> To him Africa is simply perpetual experience, exciting, amusing, alarming or delightful, which he soaks into himself through all his five senses at once, and produces again in the form of reflections, comments, songs, jokes, all in the pure Johnsonian form. Like a horse or a rose tree, he can turn the crudest and simplest form of fodder into beauty and power of his own quality. (p. 98)

The road represents Johnson's greatest achievement, for it links his creative impulse with the steady determination of Rudbeck. As complementary characters, Johnson fills the unoriginal officer with the daring to finance and construct the road according to imaginative, effective, but unorthodox methods. The project directs Johnson's seemingly inexhaustible artistic energy and fulfils at last his dream of bringing civilisation to Fada. He commits himself totally to this project, sustained by the joy of accomplishment and Rudbeck's approval:

> Johnson, in fact, has no notion that he is tired. He doesn't feel anything except music, noise, the movement of the work, the approbation and nearness of Rudbeck and Rudbeck's triumph, which is his own. He lives in this glory, which is expressed in every yell, in every obscene joke, kick, jump or swing of the machet. He does not need to think, 'Rudbeck's road, the great, the glorious, the wonder of the world, is about to be finished and I have helped to finish it.' He knows it in every muscle. It is there all the time, part of the music, the shouts, the shining sweaty backs and their rhythmic muscles, the yelling songs, the triumphant, intoxicating drums, the blue smoke of the fires, the trees toppling and crashing like cliffs, the suddenly exposed sky. (p. 176)

The same intensity that unites him with his environment as an artist now unites him with his creation, the road.

Secondly, Cary regards Johnson as a liberator. Johnson's active mind and imagination, unfettered by boredom, inspire others to free themselves from the bonds of routine. Johnson acts as an agent of change in the lives of Rudbeck, Benjamin and the road workers. He gives Rudbeck the courage to rise above the rigidity of officialdom on two separate occasions in the story. On the first, he plants the idea in Rudbeck's mind of taking funds from various votes to cover road expenses; on the second, he inspires the Britisher to execute him personally for his unpremeditated murder of Sergeant Gollup. In ignoring regulations and shooting the clerk in private instead of having him hanged in public, Rudbeck finally shatters his racist image of Johnson. He comes to see him as a human being like himself who merits the dignified death he requests. Contrary to Kettle's opinion, he shows the compassion of one man for another—not the mercy of a master for a dog.[6] He adopts what Kanu considers the only human solution possible 'in a world where judges are as guilty as the men they must judge'.[7] Cary's shift of emphasis at the end from Johnson to Rudbeck suggests a Conradian inclination, since the tragedy of one character educates another.[8] Johnson's death teaches Rudbeck the inadequacy of racist formulas.

While less dramatic, Johnson's liberation of Benjamin and the road workers seems no less remarkable than that of Rudbeck. Benjamin, the educated postal clerk, leads a voluntary life of civilised aloofness from the Fada 'pagans'. Drawing strength from Johnson's vitality at one of his parties, Benjamin temporarily loses his fear of life. Abandoning his overcaution, he starts to dance in celebration of his new freedom:

> For though he dances, he has lost not dignity, but only his stiffness, something foreign and pompous. His new dignity is graceful, strong and afraid of nothing, like all great art. (p. 210)

Not unexpectedly, Benjamin becomes an artist in this moment of freedom, for to Cary there is no creativity in captivity.

Johnson's dedication to the road is based upon his belief that civilisation will emancipate everyone from the stagnation of traditional life. The imaginative schemes he invents to recruit village labour enable these people to forget their xenophobia and take 'the first essential step out of the world of the tribe into the world of men' (p. 174). The influence he has on the self–image of the workers seems even more significant. They have so absorbed his enthusiasm for the road that they now derive a strong sense of importance from their work. In fact, they regard all those who do not build roads as lesser beings:

> For some reason, all the road gangs, even the raw pagans after they have done an hour's work on the road, despise traders like an inferior species; creatures who do not make roads, but only use them, beings without appreciation of road work; *without imagination*. (p. 177, my emphasis)

Johnson's creative force has generated a similar attitude in his men, since he has freed their minds through exposure to new experiences. He has transformed their labour into an act of adventure and work of art.

Finally, Cary presents Mister Johnson as an appreciator of other people and life itself. Although he may join Benjamin and Ajali in calling the Fada people 'dirty savages', his remarks do not betray the insecure contempt of his two friends. His 'civilisation' does not prevent him from adoring and marrying Bamu, a local girl, even though she considers him a little mad. Her refusal to become 'a government lady' does not diminish his esteem for her, because he requires little reciprocation in either his marriage or friendships. He needs only a recipient for his devotion, generosity, and gratitude; 'for him it is pleasure to admire and to create happiness' (p. 117).

Johnson's last improvisation before his death is a song of farewell and thanksgiving to nature. In it he devotes each stanza to praising an element of the sky or earth for all of the goodness it has shown him during his life. For example:

> Good-by, my worl', good-by, my father worl'.
> Carry me on you head, give me chop.
> When this fool child hear you breathe in the dark
>   he no more 'fraid
> I smell you like de honey beer in de dark night.
> I see you bress shine in de moon,
> I feel you big muscle hold me up so I no fit to fall.
> Good-by, my father, you do all ting for me, never
>   ask for nutting for yourself. (p. 243)

Johnson who takes in Africa through all five senses at once fittingly incorporates most of them into this poem. He hears, smells, sees and touches his 'father worl'' who supports, nourishes and reassures him. The generosity of the earth reflects that of Johnson himself, for to him unselfish giving is a basic part of life. The spirit of gratitude in this poem pervades all of the letters he dictates to Rudbeck before his execution. Consequently, when he ends the one to Resident Bulteel with 'I bless you and Judge Rudbeck for my happy life in de worl'', there can be no question about his sincerity. His positive appreciation of man and nature, his artistic creativity and his vital freedom have shaped his 'happy life'.

By concentrating on individuality, Cary transcends African stereotypes in portraying not only Johnson but also Ajali and Benjamin. For instance, Ajali, the clerk in Gollup's store, regularly uses his home-made key to help himself to shillings from the cash box. Cary, however, makes this dishonesty symptomatic not of Ajali's nationality but of his personality. It comes entirely from his selfishness and spite, for Ajali is an individual who deeply distrusts everyone and life itself. As an anti-life force, he serves as a foil to Johnson, the life force of the novel.[9] Since his negativity has constricted his life into mean existence, Cary often describes Ajali as an insect, crab, or scorpion:

> Cut off at the waist by the counter, on which he [Ajali] rests his fingers, he seems to lurk in the hot, stinking twilight of the shed like a scorpion in a crack, ready to spring on some prey. (p. 10)

Ajali, who finds Johnson a welcome diversion from his boredom, completely delights in Johnson's difficulties. His ill-will toward Johnson stems, in Kanu's opinion, from his dissatisfaction with life, personal insecurity and an exaggerated sense of justice.[10] His perversity provokes Johnson to anger only once when he accuses him of lying. Johnson, highly incensed, eloquently proceeds to tell Ajali the truth about himself and his contempt for life:

> 'You call me liar, I say you, yes, I'm a liar—I don' tell you the truth—I don' tell you how much Mister Tring 'gree for me because you so little small ting like stink bug. How anyone tell stink bug about de glory of God—he only make so bad stink he make you sick for belly.'
>
> Johnson's indignation is growing as he realises it. He goes off saying to himself, 'You show um a diamond, he tink um broken bottle—you show um beautiful fine horse, he tink um rock rabbit—you give um bag of gold, he tink um snake's head with troat full of yaller poison—you bring um beautiful girl, he say she dirty little goat—he creep on his belly all over everything like house lizard—he say all ting made of dirt.' (p. 113)

Johnson's images of the stink bug and house lizard complement Cary's earlier one of the equally earth-bound scorpion. Here Johnson recognises that Ajali has so completely closed himself off from the openness and beauty of life that he can no longer give, share or pleasure in the happiness of others.

In the case of Benjamin, the staid postal clerk, Cary rises above the stock image of the seemingly reliable 'native' who cannot be trusted. When Rudbeck turns the station over to his replacement, he discovers a seventeen-shilling deficiency in Benjamin's account book. Cary removes this petty embezzlement from the context of race, as M. Mahood demonstrates, by drawing Benjamin as a believably conscientious man.[11] The theft becomes simply an incident of temporary instability, perhaps caused by personal or social pressures, in the life of a normally sober individual. Benjamin's bafflement by this deviation from his usual behaviour and his suggestion that he should be fired and imprisoned for this minor offence convince the reader of his earnestness in telling Rudbeck, 'it must have been a lapse, sir' (p. 108).

Benjamin acts as a foil to Johnson because of his 'good' education, personal conservatism and moral sensibility.[12] His lack of liberation also contrasts with the freedom of Johnson, for Benjamin has entrapped himself through his over-reverence for 'civilisation'. Consequently, in an environment that inspires and fascinates Johnson, the postal clerk leads an unimaginative, unhappy, and lonely life. In spite of his desire to have a wife, he would rather remain single than marry an 'uncivilised' Fada girl:

> 'I think sometimes I take a wife, but I think these native bush girls are so ignorant and dirty. It is no good till they have some educated girls.' (p. 27)

This snobbishness and stiffness remain with him until he finally succumbs to Johnson's free spirit and begins to dance at the last party in the novel.

To Kanu, Benjamin's moral preoccupations make him 'an objectification of conscience which is lacking in the unreflective and light-travelling Johnson'.[13] As a voice of conscience, Benjamin not only warns Johnson against stealing from Sergeant Gollup, but also tells him what would happen if everyone recklessly carried out his imaginative impulses:

> 'But, Johnson, if all people did so—there would be robbery on every hand—there would be nothing but bad trouble everywhere. There would be no civilisation possible.' (p. 212)

Benjamin understands that society requires a viable balance between personal liberty and limitation. He also knows that Johnson's complete freedom and individualism will ultimately bring him to disaster. His last admonitions to his friend contain a strong sense of foreboding, for he can foresee tragedy as the outcome of Johnson's illegal actions against Gollup—'an illegal man' (p. 144).

Throughout the novel Cary uses Bamu, Johnson's wife, to dramatise the difference between traditional and modern values. Even though Johnson's proposal of marriage amounts to a statement of the 'white man's burden':

> 'Oh, Bamu, you are only a savage girl here—you do not know how happy I will make you. I will teach you to be a civilised lady and you shall do no work at all.' (p. 6)

she consistently resists his efforts to make her 'a government lady'. While Arthur Kemoli and David K. Mulwa find Bamu an extreme exaggeration of a traditional African wife, she does not really conform to the British literary image of the African woman as a submissive, hardworking drudge.[14] Despite the ease with which she assumes her wifely duties, she lacks sufficient imagination to see Johnson as a person. To her he is always the 'stranger'—someone she feeds because she has been taught that wives should do so, but someone she betrays because her tribe dislikes outsiders. While her rigidity prevents her from overcoming her stereotype of Johnson, his freedom enables him both to admire her and even to imagine her to be a loving, loyal wife.

Christopher Fyfe notes that Bamu, so beautiful and dignified in the beginning of the novel, seems bigoted and dangerous at the end when the road affects Fada.[15] This difference does not come from a personal change in Bamu, but a lack of change; she has remained static while the world of Fada has moved forward.

Joyce Cary's image of Africans in *Mister Johnson* cannot be reduced to racial generalities, since he has approached his characters as individuals. Even when he endows them with traits associated with black stereotypes, he presents them as human, not racial, qualities. Characters such as Johnson, Ajali, Benjamin and Bamu operate both on an individual level and on a universal one. They spiral up from their idiosyncracies into the larger human figures of the artist, the life–hater, the moralist and the change–resister. Indeed, the whole novel mirrors this process of enlargement, for the theme of African–Western cultural clash expands into the struggle between free and captive spirits.

Christine Garnier, a professional writer who has published several travelogues and novels set in West Africa, lived in Togo during the late 1940s and early 1950s as the wife of a French administrator. Her novel *Va-t'en avec les tiens!* is based so closely on her actual experiences in the coastal town of Anecho that it is a *roman à clef*. After its publication her husband had to be transferred to escape the reprisals of unhappy Europeans who discovered themselves as characters in the novel.[16] Her African characters are often fictionalised versions of individuals discussed in the layman's account of fetishism that she and Jean Fralon published in 1951.[17]

The plot of the novel centres around the rivalry between Doéllé, a Togolese *evoluée* and maternity nurse, and the French doctor's wife Urgèle for the love of Flavien, the French magistrate. Doéllé, who loves Flavien deeply and has been his mistress for some time, finds his infatuation with the newly arrived doctor's wife insufferable. Although Doéllé at first tries to overpower Urgèle through mental telepathy, she finally turns to traditional methods of subduing 'enemies'. She promises to marry Amérique, a man in her home village, if he will make a blood pact of friendship with the doctor's cook and then direct him to put a little bit of poison in Madame's coconut milk each morning. Urgèle, who is presented as a 'white witch', succumbs to this stronger force and gradually loses her health. When at last Doéllé sees how weak Urgèle has become, her hatred gives way to pity and she orders the poisoning to cease.

After Madame and her husband sail back to France, Doéllé resolves to marry an *évolué* and someday name a son Flavien.

Christine Garnier transcends stereotypes primarily in her portrayal of Doéllé, the main African character and the narrator of the story. Despite the stock image of black women in French colonial novels as sex objects and pet animals, she develops Doéllé as a believable individual. As the perceiving consciousness of the novel, the young *évoluée* psychologically interprets the characters she observes and analyses her own feelings. It is her frequent introspection which makes us aware of the intensity of her love, jealousy and guilt.

Even though Flavien regards Doéllé as 'a little wild animal', she sees him as a man tormented by inner conflicts and a secret but painful past.[18] In spite of his hours of sullenness and moments of sadism, she loves him and the thought of losing him is excruciating. When he falls under Urgèle's spell, she suffers, 'my heart was broken in little pieces that bled in my breast', and learns that 'love is not only a pleasure—a natural spring of joy, but also a well of sorrow' (pp. 159 and 158).

As her awareness of her love grows, so does her jealousy, for it now arises from a sense of unrequited love rather than wounded pride.

The active steps she takes to keep Flavien and Urgèle apart offer her an emotional release from both love and hate:

> I felt so strangely freed from my love and my hate, now that destiny followed the course plotted out by me. I no longer had to hesitate, worry, or think. (p. 219)

This sensation of spent passions finally permits her to pity Urgèle and forgive Flavien.

In regaining her emotional balance, Doéllé becomes increasingly guilt-ridden about having engineered Urgèle's slow poisoning. When Agbatakbato, the priest of *Hébiesso*, the god of thunder, uses his power to 'possess' others to force her sister Océa to serve as a novitiate in the cult-house, Doéllé blames herself for the young girl's misfortune:

> ... the unbearable thought came to me that the angry *Voodoo* had turned against my sister a vengeance which had been intended for me. (p. 236)

Her reference to vengeance suggests that she is starting to judge her act of jealousy as one of sin. By the time she implores Amérique to tell the cook to stop poisoning Urgèle, she perceives it as a crime:

> 'Amérique! I neither sleep nor live anymore. White people, for several days now, have looked at me in a peculiar way and I'm racked with fear. I'm losing my mind. When I meet the Nuns, I cross myself. If I see a gendarme, I want to hold out my wrists for handcuffs, and the smallest gathering in Manoho makes me afraid of a riot. I'm no longer living, I tell you. I'm no longer living. If Océa has been chosen by the fetish and has disappeared from the convent without anyone's being able to find her, it's because the gods blame me and are seeking revenge ... Amérique, isn't there still time? Go tell Kankwe not to put any more poison in the coconut milk. Madame must not die! I acted in a moment of frenzy. I've only realised today the crime that I've committed. Help me, Amérique!' (pp. 277–8)

Her strong sense of guilt seems to unify both her Western and traditional worlds, for her fear of the whites equals her conviction that she caused Océa's ill fate. Her reaction when she meets the nuns suggests that her Christian conscience bothers her just as greatly as her non–Christian one; she believes that she has offended the supreme powers of two religious systems.

The author also succeeds in rising above stereotypes in her characterisation of Doéllé as an *évoluée*. Unlike Joseph, who approaches Koffi from the outside and charges him with imitativeness and reversion, Garnier develops Doéllé psychologically, showing her progression from alienation to synthesis as a person who operates in two different cultures. At the beginning of the novel Doéllé finds herself too Westernized to accept her background and family, in spite of the social colour bar that excludes her from the white community:

> Blacks didn't interest me anymore. This hut where I had grown up naked, among clay fetishes and pythons that had escaped from the Temple, had become alien to me. And this woman enslaved to obsolete traditions, my mother, what could she be for me? I tried in vain during that night to recapture the attractions of the past: my mind was led to a cabin decorated with coral vines and rocking with the latest music. While drinking palm–wine with Amérique and Océa, I thought of the champagne that Urgèle and Flavien were drinking in the demonstration garden [of the agricultural station]. I trembled all over with an excited yet sad impatience at the thought of soon being near white people again. These whites who barred me from their parties and made me suffer. (p. 76)

She has lost both her sense of solidarity with blacks in general and with her relatives in particular. Her description of her mother first as a 'woman enslaved to obsolete traditions' and secondly as 'my mother' indicates that her Westernisation has interfered with her filial love. Her fascination with whites has made her judge her mother severely as a seemingly useless tie with a childhood that has lost its charm. Her attitude towards whites displays ambivalence, however, for her admiration of them has been scarred by their racial discrimination.

Although Doéllé returns home for important family occasions, she does not re–establish close emotional ties with her mother until Océa's subjugation by the priest of *Hébiesso*. This event constitutes a family crisis, since a novitiate in this cult must remain completely cloistered for three years. Mutual concern for Océa and shared tears reunite Doéllé with her mother emotionally. It is this incident which inspires the Catholic nurse to pray to her ancestral gods as well as the Christian one for Océa's protection.

Doéllé's new relationship with her mother and her reliance on traditional religion continue to grow, when the priest sends Océa to another cult–house as a punishment for shaming the local convent by her pregnancy. The discovery of Océa's body weeks later floating on a raft in the lagoon confirms Doéllé's belief that her 'criminal plot' caused her sister's death (p. 291). Her grief then joins that of her mother and Océa's fiancé, making them one in a bond of sorrow and love.

These events, which give Doéllé a new understanding of her family and her culture, help her integrate her Western assimilation with her tribal heritage. Her description of herself at the beginning of the book as a person who has been 'without a family or homeland, since the promises of their civilisation threw me off course', bears little resemblance to the cultural hybrid she finally becomes. By the end of the novel, her dreams of Océa's death arouse a mixed religious and cultural response:

> At night I hear howling in my dreams and I don't know whether it's the God of the Missions reproaching me or the fetishes barking in my ear; I wonder if it's my conscience that cries or the *Voodoo* that threatens. (p. 295)

Doéllé's emulation of the whites has been tempered by their rejection, forcing her to admit the impossibility of operating completely in their world. Garnier portrays the nurse's increasing recognition of her culture as a gradual process of awareness rather than reversion by presenting the customs of the Mina in southern Togo as facets of a different world view instead of 'proofs' of 'savagery'. Much of this ethnographic material, particularly the information about Océa's life in the cult–house and the blood pact between Amérique and Kankwe, can be found in her book *Le Fetichisme en Afrique noire (Togo–Cameroun)*.[19] The author's placement of authentic details in a setting that conveys the cohesiveness of rural life prevents their misinterpretation by Western readers.

Doéllé's greater appreciation of her African roots changes her vision of herself and her future. She abandons her secret dreams that her assimilation will make the French forget her colour, since all of the colonialists in the novel adopt the attitude 'after all, you're only a black. Go back to your own kind!' (p. 301). She now knows that she will marry not a white man but 'a man of my own station in life, some African doctor', and hopes that some day her children will experience the social equality that Europeans have always denied her (p. 301).

Both Doéllé and Mister Johnson are so credible that the reader finds universal qualities in them. Paradoxically, it is their uniqueness which enables the reader to do so, permitting him to see in Johnson the artist whose freedom and imagination are thwarted by conventional society and in Doéllé the unrequited lover who moves through remorse from jealousy to forgiveness.

NOTES

1. Joyce Cary, *The Case for African Freedom and Other Writings on Africa* (Austin: Univ. of Texas Press, 1962) p. 54.
2. Arnold Kettle, *An Introduction to the English Novel*, vol. ii (London: Hutchinson Univ. Library, 1967) pp. 161–5. Frederick R. Karl, *The Contemporary English Novel* (New York: The Noonday Press, 1962) p. 137.
3. Killam, *Africa*, pp. 162–3.
4. Joyce Cary, *Mister Johnson* (New York; Berkley Pub. Corp., 1964) p. 161. All subsequent page references will be to this edition and will appear immediately in the text.
5. Sheka Hassan Kanu, *A World of Everlasting Conflict: Joyce Cary's View of Man and Society* (Ibadan: Ibadan Univ. Press, 1974) p. 74.
6. Kettle, p. 165.
7. Kanu, pp. 90–1.
8. Michael C. Echeruo, *Joyce Cary and the Novel of Africa* (New York: Africana Pub. Co., 1973) p. 122.
9. Golden L. Larsen, *The Dark Descent: Social Change and Moral Responsibility in the Novels of Joyce Cary* (London: Michael Joseph, 1965) p. 79.
10. Kanu, p. 75.
11. M. M. Mahood, *Joyce Cary's Africa* (London: Methuen & Co., 1964) p. 184.
12. Kanu, pp. 76–7.
13. Ibid., p. 77.
14. Arthur Kemoli and David K. Mulwa, 'The European Image of Africa and the African', *Busara*, vol. ii, no. 2 (1969) p. 52.
15. Christopher Fyfe, 'The Colonial Situation in Mister Johnson', *Modern Fiction Studies*, vol. ix, no. 3 (Autumn 1963) p. 229.
16. Macalister C. Cairns, 'The African Colonial Society in French Colonial Novels', *Cahiers d'Etudes Africaines*, vol. ix, no. 34 (1969) p. 186.
17. Christine Garnier and Jean Fralon, *Le Fetichisme en Afrique noire (Togo–Cameroun)* (Paris: Payot, 1951).
18. Christine Garnier, *Va-t'en avec les tiens!* (Paris: Bernard Grasset, Editeur, 1951)

p. 74. All subsequent page references will be to this edition, and will follow immediately in the text. This translation and all subsequent ones are mine.
19. A factual account of these events may be found on pages 76–80 and 135–144 of this book.

PART TWO: AFRICANS LOOK AT EUROPEANS

6 Origins of European Stereotypes in West African Novels

If one wishes to examine the attitudes towards whites that have most shaped their image in contemporary anglophone and francophone West African novels, he must turn to the oral literature of the past 150 years. There both a spectrum of stereotypes and a pattern of ambivalence will be discovered. The mixture of admiration and resentment in the African view of the European results from colonialism, for to the colonised the coloniser served as a model as well as an oppressor.

Oral literature with its explanations of the origin of racial inequality offers the earliest awareness of white domination, power and wealth. In his study of African political myths dealing with Europeans, Georges Balandier has charted a dynamic progression which successively involves: (1) the recognition of the fact of colonialism, (2) the reaction against colonialism, and (3) the justification of independence.[1] His contention would be that the following Mangbetu story acknowledges the white man's position of superiority within colonialism and that it probably arose during the early days of European–Mangbetu contact:

> The first human beings were looking for water. God gave it to them, but only one of them thought of thanking him. God rewarded him and made him the ancestor of the white men.[2]

For many tribes, works such as this one helped to explain not only why the white was so wealthy, but also why he had conquered the black with so much ease. Depending upon the cause given for European material superiority, these stories may be classified as either (1) black transgression, (2) black choice, or (3) white chicanery. The first type demonstrates a neglect or denial of tribal values; the second points to character weakness; the third blames European domination on white duplicity.

In her comprehensive study of thirty-seven black inequality stories, Görög has drawn examples of these three types from anthologies of sub-Saharan folklore published between 1705 and 1967. Most of her source material, however, was gathered by missionaries in West and Central Africa from 1880 to 1914, substantiating Balandier's interpretation of such stories as an early confrontation with white supremacy. Among her illustrations of the black transgression theme is this story collected by Father Trilles from the Gabonese Fang around the turn of the century:

> God commanded the two sons of the first man to perform a laborious task. The Black (the oldest son) refused to obey the order, but the White applied himself to the task, and God gave him the wealth which would otherwise have fallen to the Black. God, moved by the sadness of the Black, gave him another chance to save himself. He commanded him to go down a mountain without looking behind him. But the Black broke this commandment and he suffered forever because of it.[3]

This story, which combines a transgression with a test, is unusual because it awards a second chance to the black. The plot is essentially built upon a reversal, since the black son as the older initially commands more privileges than his white brother, but forfeits them by refusing to undertake the burdensome task God requires of him. It is quite possible that the punishment delivered against the black implies perpetual poverty, for a second Fang story gathered by Father Trilles, 'The Legend of the Noas', concludes explicitly with the curse, 'The White Man will always be white and the Black Man black, the White Man always rich, the Black Man always poor.'[4]

Often in both black transgression and black choice stories Europeans are rewarded with knowledge or literacy as shown by the Kaguru Noah analogue recorded by T. O. Beidelman in Tanzania.[5] In this story an aging father of twin sons—one 'ruddy' and one 'dark'—tries to teach them the significance of divination. While the white one listens carefully, the black one acts disrespectfully and mocks the teachings of his father. As a result, when the father later calls his sons to him on his death bed, he says that he will bestow upon the 'ruddy' son whatever he wants, but that the 'dark' one will receive nothing:

> Then the ruddy son said, 'I want you to give me every kind of knowledge'. And every kind of knowledge was given to him, but nothing was given to the other one. Now today the ruddy child['s descendants] are the Europeans who have much knowledge and we [Africans] are the dark ones without much knowledge.[6]

Here the brothers begin as equals, for there is no mention of the seniority of the twins. The irony of this story is that the European succeeds as a consequence of being a more conscientious Kaguru than his African brother. As a black transgression story, it cleverly conserves traditional values at the same time that it recognises the higher social and economic status of the European. Moreover, no real moral superiority is accorded to the European, since it is his excellent Kaguru behaviour that gains him his reward and establishes the image of the European as a man of knowledge.

The second type of black inequality stories, those dealing with the theme of black choice, appear rather frequently in anthologies of West African folklore. Their plots typically involve two brothers, one black and one white, who are asked either by a deity or their parents to choose between two objects, one big and one small, or two piles of objects, one pertaining to agriculture or raw materials and the other to literacy. Invariably the black as the favourite son makes his selection first, opting for the larger container or the heap of farm implements, and thereby condemns himself to the life of a subsistence cultivator. The white then takes what remains—paper, pencils, and books—and achieves technological knowledge and power over the black through default. Although the unwise decision of the black is usually ascribed to greed, Görög regards the contest as a kind of intelligence test.[7]

The stereotype of the European as the 'man of the book' is longstanding, for next to skin colour what differentiated him most noticeably from non-literate Africans was his ability to read and write. The Livingstones pointed to this image of the white man in their remarks, 'our books, too, were objects of admiration. The idea that enters their minds is that books are our instruments of divination.'[8]

The main characteristics of black choice stories are illustrated in the following selection collected prior to 1887 by Alfred Burdon Ellis from the Twi–speaking people in Ghana:

> ... three black men and three white, each with a woman of his own colour, were made by a god, who laid before them a covered calabash and a folded piece of paper, and told them they were to choose which they would have. The blacks had the first choice and chose the calabash, thinking it would contain everything they wanted; but on opening it they found only a piece of iron, a little gold, and some metals the uses of which they were unacquainted with. The paper fell to the lot of the whites, who, on opening it, found that it contained directions for making everything. The god, disgusted at the avarice of the blacks in having chosen the calabash, conducted the whites to seashore, taught them how to build ships, and sent them away in one, telling them that they should become masters of the blacks through the very gift which the latter had spurned.[9]

The ships introduce another common element of these stories, the temporary separation of the races. As shown here the blacks usually remain where they are or head inland into the forest and the whites cross the ocean, later returning as the masters of the blacks. In accordance with convention, the metals in this story are primarily materials which only the whites will know how to exploit.

A Neyo variant of this theme was collected by the colonial administrator Georges Thomann near Sassandra, Ivory Coast:

> The story goes that Tapi, the Sky, made a man and a woman come down to the earth. Later they had two children—a black and a white son. The parents then said: 'We are going to test the intelligence of our sons' and with that intention in mind, they prepared a well–laden table, placing water, a towel, and soap near by. Then they called the two children to come eat. The black son washed his hands without soap and wiped them on his cloth wrapper, while the white one used the soap and took the towel to wipe his fingers. Then the two came and helped themselves at the table. The black settled himself on the ground to eat his share of the food, but the white sat in a chair and ate with the help of a fork. When they were finished, they left the table. The parents then led them to the river where they saw a steamship and a canoe. The black went to the boats first, passed

the steamship, then got into the canoe and sat down. The white then came, climbed aboard the steamship, put the propellor in motion, and the ship began to move. The black couldn't do the same thing with his canoe, so he moved forward laboriously with the help of a paddle. When they were returning, the parents told the black to paddle over next to the ship. He obeyed, but was so frightened by the sight of the ship, that he fled to a distant country. Later the white brother went to join his brother again, carrying with him as gifts cloth, tobacco, and manufactured goods. The black in turn gave him a steer, a sheep, and some chickens, saying 'Here are some animals in exchange for what I've bought from you.' The white replied: 'But I haven't sold you a thing; these are gifts that I've given you.' But the black wouldn't hear of it. Then his brother became annoyed and told him, 'I wanted to give you a gift, but you wouldn't accept it that way. From now on, even though you're my brother, whenever I bring you anything, it will be for commerce.'

That's why the whites import merchandise into our country and we have trade relations with them.[10]

Here intelligence is equated with being Westernised and a value judgment is made in favour of things European at the expense of traditional Neyo manners and transport. The charge of black ignorance underlies the African brother's fear of the steamship and misinterpretations of his brother's gifts. In keeping with the pattern of separation, the black goes off to an agricultural country, the white to an industrial one. At the end the white brother assumes the role usually reserved for a deity or parent by prophesying about their future relations. The explicit and implied criticisms of the black brother suggest that this story arose after more contact with whites and *la mission civilisatrice* than the Twi example which only accused Africans of cupidity.

The stories that offer the greatest amount of African self-assertion are those that view white chicanery as the cause of white dominance. As double-edged works, they simultaneously recognise the power of the white and protest against his unscrupulousness. They generally are analogous to the Biblical tale of Jacob and Esau, since they contain two brothers who are charged by a parent to perform a deed, such as hunting, in order to receive a reward. Often the white brother deceives his father by substituting the carcass of a domestic animal for a wild one, thereby robbing the black sibling who returns later of his rightful recompense. In these narratives the black who respects tradition and accomplishes the required task is patently cheated by his brother. Thus, the theme of white chicanery shifts the emphasis from self-accusation to predestination and white deception, for the African is a victim and not a sinner.

An outstanding example of this kind of story was recounted to Ruth Finnegan in Sierra Leone by the Limba storyteller Suriba (Never-tire) Konteh.[11] In 'The White and Black Brothers' the father of both a black and white son favours the black one, while the mother favours the white. The father, wishing to test his sons, writes a book which explains 'how to make a ship, aeroplane, money, how to make everything' and prepares various plants and farm implements.[12] The father's desire to give the book to his black son is undone by his partial blindness:

> Now their father could not see well. He could not see the children clearly. He said, 'Child, you, when you go to hunt, do not go very far.' He just turned round, he caught a sheep, he killed it. He [white one] came, he said, 'Father, I have brought meat. I went to hunt for it.' Well, that pleased his father. Because he could not see well, he thought he was lifting down the hoe to give the white one. Behold it was the book he took. 'Take the book for me.' The wife took the book. He said, 'Give it to the child, the one who brought the meat.' He was given it. [It is not clear if it was the hoe or the child that the father mistook. In any case the book was given to the wrong son]. He was not afraid to peep at it. He started reading it. He started seeing the things, how to make the aeroplane, how to make everything, how to make a ship, he saw it in the book.
>
> The black one came. He said, 'Father, greetings. What have you kept for me? I have killed a bird. It is what I have brought.' He said, 'Ah, my child, you are left as a foolish man. Well, take this hoe. Here is a basket, rice is in it. Millet is in it. Groundnuts are in it. Everything that you use when you go to work is there. But you are likely always to be left behind. He is more than you. Everything, if you want to get it, you have to ask your companion, the white one.'
>
> You see us, the black people, we are left in suffering. The unfairness of our birth makes us remain in suffering. That is why they want to send us to learn the writing of the Europeans. But our mother did not agree, she did not love us. She loved the white

people. She gave him the book. There they saw how to make everything in happiness [without suffering]. They were able to do that and to surpass us the black people . . .

If you see the Europeans, everything they are doing, they have to put a black man there. He is a clerk; he sits in the store, he does everything. This is the way. Yesterday we were full brothers with them. We come from one descent, the same mother, the same father, but the unfairness of our birth, that is why we are different. We will not know what you know unless we learn from you. We are brothers of the same parents, that is why you learn from books, to teach us black people so that we may know. Why we are alike—we are full brothers.[13]

In a departure from other versions, the narrator accuses the father of 'wanting to act unfairly' in his desire to give the book to his black son rather than to whoever first returns with the game. The father's advice to the wrong son and the confidence with which the white one approaches and reads the book affirm the idea that he is predestined to be literate, knowledgeable and wealthy. The black brother's ill fortune in the hunt, an exception to the convention, serves to establish subsistence farming as his destiny. The ending expresses the stereotypes that literacy is the source of white superiority and that whites lead a life of ease in which blacks do all the work. The story exhibits some ambivalence, however, for although the white commits an act of dishonesty, Suriba concludes that the difference between the brothers stems from the unfairness of their birth and their mother rather than trickery. The European, whose full fraternity obliges him to share his 'book learning' with his less fortunate brother, consequently becomes an educational model for the African.

A more standard handling of white chicanery in Jacob and Esau analogues can be seen in these excerpts from the Nigerian Ekoi story entitled 'How Black and White Men Came on Earth', told by Ojong of Oban:

> Meanwhile the white boy thought, 'Why should I trouble to go out hunting?' So he took his mother's goat and skinned it. Then he brought it to his father and said, 'Here is an antelope which I have just killed in the bush.'

and

After a time the black boy came back with a fine antelope (Naun) which he had killed, but, when he laid it down before his father, the latter said: 'I have already accepted enough fresh meat from my white son, and to him have I given the hunter's reward.'[14]

Here injustice prevails instead of predestination, for the white son clearly cheats his black brother out of his merited reward. The disrespectful white actually deceives both of his parents, since he first steals from his mother then lies to his father.

An even stronger statement of white chicanery comes across in this Ashanti explanation of the Portuguese enslavement of Africans which moves away from the Biblical analogue altogether:

'When the Portuguese first landed, the natives betook themselves to the forest. When the white man had put off again the natives crept cautiously back to the beach. To their great surprise they found there a basin of rum. One of them, by name Mbura, tested some, and finding that it was sweet, drank as much as he could and became intoxicated. Others did the same, and when many of them were helpless the boatman returned and carried them off. On account of the rum being tasted by Mbura, we call rum in Fantee *Mbura–nsa*—i.e. Mbura's wines.'[15]

In this case European cunning exploits the Africans' unfamiliarity with rum left on the beach as a snare. Rum, a common symbol of the European, occurs frequently in plastic art as well as folklore, especially among the coastal ethnic groups who were most deeply affected by the slave trade. Unlike the book, rum has pejorative connotations because of the demoralisation it brought to Africans.

In contrast to these stories of black inferiority are those that celebrate black superiority by defining the negative characteristics of Europeans. The whites in these narratives, despite their treachery, boasting, and hypocrisy, are all eventually outwitted by blacks. The following tale which exposes the white man's pride and bragging, was collected by Heli Chatelain in Angola before 1894:

The White Man and the Negro

Two men, a white man and a negro, had a discussion.

The white man said: 'I, in my house there is lacking nothing. I have all (things).' The negro said: 'Untruth! In thy house, I look for a thing, I do not find it.' The white man said: 'You, negroes, you lack all things; I have to look for nothing.'

The negro assented; went to his house. He spent a month. He wove his mat; he is sewing it. He arrives in the middle of the mat; the cords give out. There is no more a place where he can take the dry cords. He says: 'How shall I do? I will go to the house of the white man, that he give me the cords, that I may finish the mat.'

He arose; arrives at the white man's, says: 'Sir, I am in need (at the place) whence I come.' The white man says: 'What needest thou?' He says: 'I was weaving a mat; it gave out. I said, 'I will go to the house, in which are all things; the white man that he give me a few cords, that I may finish my mat.'

The white man looks at him; he laughs. He goes into the store; he looks in it: there are no cords in it. He says: 'Negro, thou art lucky.' He takes a hundred macutas; he gives them to the negro.

The discussion, that the white man had with the negro, the negro won (it), the white man lost (it).[16]

This tale humorously reveals the white man's braggadacio and suggests his cultural chauvinism in assuming that owning Western objects is tantamount to having everything. The giving of cash to the African reinforces the stereotype of European as rich and money-oriented, for a hundred macutas serve as his admission that the African has proved him wrong.

The Ekoi of Eastern Nigeria and West Cameroun have a story which accentuates European wealth, avarice and temper:

The Treasure House in the Bush

Obassi Osaw had two sons. The name of the first was Oro, and of the Second Agbo. When their father died, Oro took all the property, while Agbo remained in the sky as a poor washerman. One day the latter said to his wife, 'There is no food either for you or me. I must go into the bush and hunt, that we may not die of hunger.' He went along a road which brought him down to earth, and led him at length to a part of the bush where a house was standing by itself. He wondered whose it might be, and crept round behind some bushes to watch unseen.

Soon some white people came through the bush close to where

the hunter was hidden. He saw them open the door, carry forth a great treasure, and then lock up again.

When they had gone, Agbo crept out from his hiding place, found a way to enter the house, and took from it as much treasure as he could carry. This he bore off to the sky. When his wife saw what he had brought she said, 'Where did you get all this?' He answered 'From a house in the bush where white people keep it.'[17]

After Agbo robs the Treasure House a few more times, Oro becomes curious about his brother's newfound wealth. Agbo finally tells him the secret and they go to the Treasure House together. However, Oro is not satisfied with only one visit:

When night came, Agbo grew anxious because his brother did not return. All night he waited, and, when day dawned, set out by the way which Oro had taken. On and on he went till he came to the house in the bush. There, oh, terrible sight! he found the fragments of his brother's body lying before the door. He collected every bit, and carried them sadly away. After a while he sought out a tailor and said, 'Here is the body of a man who got cut to pieces in the bush. Can you sew it together again? If you will do this for me I will pay you richly.' The tailor answered, 'I will try what I can do'.

When the owner of the treasure returned and found all the pieces gone he was very angry. He thought, 'Who can have carried away the dead man's body, and what can have been done with it?' In his turn he also went to the tailor and asked, 'Has anyone brought you pieces to mend?' The tailor replied, 'Yes, a man named Agbo brought some.'

The owner asked, 'Who is Agbo? I do not know him.' One of his servants answered, 'I know who he is, and can find out all about him.' (pp. 390–1)

The servant then befriends Agbo and paints all of his houseposts white so that his master can easily identify Agbo and all the other members of his compound. Agbo's son, who has already warned his father of this servant's treachery, whitewashes all of the houseposts in the village:

When the white man came early in the morning with a great

following, he found the whole town painted alike, so he could not find the house which he sought, and was forced to return home without doing anything. He blamed his servant because the latter had failed to keep his promise ... (p. 391)

The servant, however, persuades the white man to lend him warriors whom he smuggles into Agbos' compound in palm oil casks. Agbo shows great hospitality to his new friend and insists that he spend the night. The son, recognising his father's great danger, cuts the servant's throat while he is asleep, then bores a hole in each cask and fills it with boiling water. The next morning Agbo is outraged by the murder of his friend and drags his son before the judge. When the casks are opened and there is clear evidence of the servant's intentions the judge acquits Agbo's son and his father rewards him for having saved his life.

The details of this story provide some insight into the African image of the European. For example, the fact that the Treasure House stands by itself in the bush points to European aloofness. As a consequence of the white men's great wealth, there is less of a sense of wrong-doing attached to Agbo's thefts, for the Europeans seem to have far more then they need and Agbo is initially motivated by hunger. On the other hand, Oro who already owns property suffers because of his greed and fascination with wealth. His dismemberment stands as a commentary on both his own greed and the anger of Europeans. The European's outrage over the removal of Oro's fragments suggests a fear of Oro's possible resurrection to rob again, and illustrates the white man's possessiveness of his wealth.

The white man's dependence upon his servant as a spy, providing information about Agbo and arranging his employer's revenge, seems to emphasise the white's unfamiliarity with Africans as well as expedience. While the counter-trick is a common motif in world folklore, the painting of all the houseposts by Agbo's son may be a correlative of the stereotype that Europeans think all Africans look alike. A measure of the extent to which the servant has been corrupted by the white man can be seen in his equation of loyalty to his employer with the betrayal of Agbo.

A subgroup of black superiority stories criticises the European obliquely by replacing him with a Westernised African. Often a contest between traditional African and modern European life styles occurs in which the pretension of the *évolué* is derided as an extension of white pomposity. This same device of indirect censure also arises frequently in proverbs that ridicule Africans for imitating the behaviour of Europeans. A Bandi tale entitled 'The Two Fastest Men in the World', collected by John Milbury–Steen in Liberia, centres around Belebele, a traditional hunter, and Vulai, a Westernised 'book man', or *kwi*, who hear of each other's reputation for speed and come together to demonstrate their prowess:

> Once upon a time: They were going and it was on the road to Belebele's home they were going, understand? Then it was Belebele who was just crossing a small river, or a middle–size one. He had crossed it before he and his friend met. This middle–size river had a bridge across it. That bridge was one stick. And as for this stick, it was dry wood and old. When they reached there, that man who was Belebele, the hunter, was in front. They were on the road to his town. He said, 'Let me pass in front.' He passed in front and stepped on the log quickly and crossed the river and came down on the other side. He sat over there waiting for his friend, understand? Oh, as for his friend, all these *kwi* clothes he had on made him heavier than his friend. When he came and reached the middle of the river he had just then reached the middle when this log said 'Crack!' Splitting was what it was doing, see. When it just said, 'Crack!' he was able to take his hat off his head, take his *kwi* eyes off his eyes, take off his neck–catcher, take off his shirt–under–a–shirt, take off his shirt–over–a–shirt (that's a robe they put on their backs, the *kwi* people, you know, you yourself, not so?) take that off, and was able to take off his trousers–over–trousers and trousers–under–trousers and was able to take the shoes off his feet and his foot–clothes, taking it all off, and the watch on his wrist and everything in his hand, and put it all in a handkerchief and tie it tight and throw it on the bank–all before he hit the water! As soon as the log said 'Crack!' that's what happened before he hit the water. He said, 'Boy, you saw that?' The other one said, 'Yes.' They were going.
>
> Then, they arrived, this one and his friend who was a hunter. Then they saw a deer on the road on their way going. Just as his friend said the 'd' in 'Deer'–he just said 'D . . .' and the '. . . eer' hadn't even been added yet—even then he heard the sound of a gun, you understand? He shot the gun: boom! He laid down this gun, laid it down, took a knife, went running far, jumped on the deer, killed it, cut it up, put it in a hamper, tied it tight, put it on his back, adjusted the shoulder straps on his back, and was

coming just as he and the gun shot were about to meet. It was still flying! He said to the bullet, 'Oops, excuse me, please, and let me pass. If you stay on that course, you'll kill me. But what are you still doing in the air? Here's the deer meat already in my hand. Just go wherever you're going.'

Once upon a time: Oh, those were two fast people. Of the two—this is the question—who was more powerful than his friend?[18]

The question at the end seems to have been answered by the narrator, since he apparently favours Belebele's faster and more functional feat. Using overemphasis as an expression of disapproval, he makes his implied criticism of the unsuitability of Vulai's European clothing more explicit when it causes the bridge to break. Vulai's proof of quickness amounts to a literal stripping away of his pretensions. It is a traditional African bridge that humbles him into nakedness before he lands in the water.

On the contrary, Belebele's demonstration of speed involves the survival skill of hunting. The Bandi, who practise subsistence farming and rarely have a plentiful supply of meat, would naturally regard Belebele's deed which helps to sustain life as more important than Vulai's. Vulai's Western bookishness and dress serve no purpose in the bush, failing to bring him food or even keep him dry. This story not only reasserts the traditional values of Bandi life, even to the extreme that Belebele slays the deer with a Bandi knife rather than a Western gun, but also comically teaches that in the Bandi environment one must act like a Bandi.

West African oral narratives which deal with Europeans directly or indirectly whether they deal with black inferiority or superiority must be viewed more as a continuum than a polarity, since they integrate a considerable amount of admiration with detestation in their identification of 'European traits'.

Proverbs, as a major didactic genre within the oral literary tradition, have served as another significant conveyor of African attitudes towards Europeans. Originally inspired by the increased European presence in West Africa under colonialism, such proverbs still help individuals interpret and interact successfully with the white man while discouraging the undue adoption of his ways.

Robert S. Rattray devotes a whole chapter to 'Strangers. Europeans and Europe' in his anthology of Ashanti sayings. Although he provides helpful linguistic and grammatical notes for most of these proverbs, he largely refrains from analysing their meanings. The following ones emphasise European wealth, employing both 'Europe' and 'Europeans' as synonyms for material riches:

—All men would like to go to Europe, it is the opportunity they lack.
—If any one had knowledge previous to his birth that he was going to have to suffer from poverty, then he would have gone to the white men that he might be born of them.
—When your mother lives in Africa and your father in Europe, and when there is a thing you want, you do not have to wait for it.[19]

C. A. Akrofi observes in his discussion of the Twi variant of the first proverb that it means 'all men desire good things, but they are not obtained by all'.[20] The second one shows how completely the white man is identified with affluence, for poverty among Europeans is inconceivable. The last one further accentuates these fabled fortunes, claiming that if one has close access to Europeans and their money, virtually all of one's material desires will be fulfilled.

Three other proverbs clearly demonstrate an Ashanti deflation of the white man's mystique by reminding people that he is dependent upon his translators and is just as subject to human frailty and fatality as anyone else:

—It is the native who knows English who directs the white man to praise (and whom to blame).
—A feast uncovers a European's wooden leg.
—The white man who lives in the castle, when he dies he lies in the ground.[21]

The white man's, especially the colonial officer's, inability to speak a local language forms a major part of the oral as well as written literary image of the European as culturally insensitive. This proverb quite accurately depicts the initial stages of colonialism, when the interpreter was counted upon by both the coloniser and the colonised as a communications broker. He was thought to wield great influence over whites, since no colonial authority could exercise his power without the services of his translator.

The second proverb refers to a feast followed by 'a big drink' and means that intoxication can reveal the normally hidden flaws of the European.[22] The association of the white with heavy drinking, often as a means of coping with life in the tropics, prevails as well in the modern West African literary image of the European.

According to Rattray, the phrase 'the white man who lives in the castle' refers to the Governor, while the term 'white man' literally means 'dirt', since the Ashanti who first observed whites said they looked like the colour of white dirt or clay.[23] Here death, the great humbler, condemns the Europeans to the fate of all men.

The Yoruba in Western Nigeria have also developed proverbs about Europeans that exhibit some of the ambivalence evident among the Ashanti. On the one hand, we find among Burton's quotations from the 1852 work of Bishop Samuel Crowther:

—The fame of the white man spreads throughout the world.
—The white man is the father of merchants: (want of) money is the father of disgrace.

while on the other we encounter:

—Though the white man's gauze came all the way over the sea, yet what cloth may be compared to cloth of Akese cotton?[24]

The first one acknowledges the pervasiveness of the European's influence and implies a laudatory awareness of his power. The second one weighs his riches against the pennilessness that brings disgrace. Although it is possible to interpret the second part as an expression of white bankruptcy, it probably deals with the plight of the African without money whose economy has been converted from barter to cash by the European. The third saying asserts Yoruba pride and is applied to individuals who are outstanding in either action or ability.[25]

In a more recent collection, Bernth Lindfors lists two Yoruba proverbs that relate directly to Europeans or European acculturation:

—The Whiteman made the pencil, he also made the eraser.
—A person who knows English never dies at the place of his birth.[26]

Lindfors claims that the first one, which means whoever has the power to make a law also has the power to change it, does not refer to the duplicity of colonialists, because his informant has never heard it used that way.[27] His argument is not totally convincing, however, since the existence of white chicanery stories points at least in longer narrative genres to an oral literary image of white cunning and self-interest. This proverb obviously accuses Europeans of some inconsistency and arbitrariness. He suggests that the second one, based on the greater mobility of the educated in comparison with the uneducated, was coined in the last thirty years.[28] Also implicit in this proverb is the understanding that the migrations of the educated away from home fracture the traditional cohesiveness of extended families.

A Hausa saying, reminiscent of the Yoruba one about the white man and the pencil, satirises European craftiness, '"Perhaps" prevents the European from telling a lie.'[29] Unlike Lindfors, Kirk-Greene regards it as a lampoon of the method Europeans use to remain uncommitted, so that technically they never break a promise.[30] This Hausa charge that whites are obsessed with keeping their word seems to counterbalance the European stereotype that Africans never fulfil promises or honour contracts.

The following proverbs were all obtained from a Hausa informant, Mr Bala Muhammad. The fact that Kirk-Greene has included only one saying about Europeans in his authoritative work on Hausa proverbs, while Mr Muhammad could easily think of several, suggests that most examples of this kind of proverb have yet to be collected.

—The white man never rides a donkey. (Among the Hausa only peasants ride donkeys.)
—The white man's urine knows no gossip. (The white man, who does not speak Hausa, never talks about himself. In Hausa, urine is a metaphor for one's personal business.)
—The Son of Tasalla can even write from left to right. ('The Son of Tasalla', a Hausa praise epithet for 'lucky born', is applied to the white man who can do anything—even write from left to right—rather than in the Arabic fashion of the Islamic Hausa.)
—The white man's urine knows nothing about grain from the market. (Since a white man is never seen purchasing or eating grain from the market, the people marvel that he still stays alive.)
—The white man has nothing to do with breaking wind.

(Breaking wind is shameful in Hausa culture. The white man, who does not eat Hausa food, cannot be associated with the effect that it apparently has on the Hausa.)
—The white man is the king of the world. (The world in Hausa belief is surrounded by the seas. The white man has conquered them through his superior technological knowledge.)[31]

The image of the white man which emerges here is one of a great but curious person who stands apart from Hausa culture and society. The first one recognises the status and wealth of the European. The three proverbs that claim that the white man does not talk about himself, eat Hausa food, or break wind are all observations of European aloofness. In a strongly communal and collective society isolation as an anti–social behaviour becomes one of the major sources of white peculiarity. The familiar theme of white literacy undergoes an interesting variation in the third saying, since the Hausa have long been acquainted with reading and writing in Arabic. Here the amazing fact is not that the European can write, but that he can break tradition, do it backwards, and still make sense of it. The emphasis on technology in the last proverb, another standard element of the African view of the white man, conventionally attributes his superiority to inventiveness and material knowledge.

Some proverbs that represent European cruelty and haughtiness have been recorded among the Jabo people in Liberia and the Limba in Sierra Leone respectively:

—White people say: one doesn't die of buttocks.
—Do not walk in a European way with a loin cloth.[32]

The Jabo proverb, according to George Herzog, is ascribed to the whites, since the Jabo do not severely beat children or adults as a punishment for minor offences.[33] Because many Liberians worked in neighbouring colonies as migrant labourers, the white man's authoritarianism was widely known through either first or second hand experience. Currently among the Jabo, this saying is used to demonstrate to a child who has been punished by an adult or to a person who has been offended by someone that his suffering is not as serious as he thinks. The second proverb charges the Limba who imitate the self–possessed walk of the European with affectation. Finnegan's informant explains that among the Limba, 'a white man is associated with pomposity, pride, and wealth; and it is ridiculous for anyone without the same amount of wealth to put on the airs of the European'.[34]

The phenomenon observed in West African oral literature of viewing the white with both admiration and detestation is also apparent in Gustav Jahoda's study of Ghanaian stereotypes of Europeans shortly before independence.[35] While his sample group, which included middle and secondary school students as well as educated and uneducated adults, generally displayed a mixed attitude towards whites, their favourable responses outnumbered the unfavourable ones. Among the middle school students, whites were described as all looking alike, speaking English and being both reserved and lazy. Even though these students also regarded them as exploitative, weaker and less virile than Africans, they credited whites with good manners, punctuality, honesty, cleanliness, technology and intelligence. Secondary school students commended Europeans for their attention to their children's questions and their promptness, but complained about their social isolation, privileged position and discrimination against Africans.

Adults who were asked what they had been told about whites during childhood painted a complex image of them as both good and bad; kind and cruel; wonderful magicians and terrible exploiters; civilisers and bogeymen. All of the adults, whether literate or not, rated progress and education as the greatest benefits brought by the white and immorality (mainly prostitution and promiscuity) and drinking (often mentioned with smoking, gambling and ballroom dancing) as the worst evils. Eighty per cent of the informants said that Europeans held a low opinion of Africans, remarking:

—They think Africans are subhuman because of their colour.
—They think we are black monkeys.
—Some regard Africans as a curious set of people, while others regard them as an inferior race.
—They treat us like children.
—Whites are too proud. They think we don't mind because we don't insult them.
—They think that Africans are not intelligent and that without their help Africans would be helpless.
—They think we are primitive, disregard us, and don't give us promotions.

—Whites think all Africans are 'boys'. . . .
—Whites think Africans are inferior but keep flattering us since they benefit.[36]

Jahoda found 'that in general personal contact was significantly associated with dislike,' since practically all areas of black/white interaction under colonialism involved black subordination to white superiors.[37] In attributing most of the positive stereotypes of Europeans to the idealistic image of the British fostered in school textbooks, he overemphasised education as the source of the Ghanaian ambivalence towards whites.[38] Since he has overlooked the oral literary image of whites, he appears to be unaware of the extent to which the approach/avoidance syndrome existed before the establishment of mass education in West Africa.

René Maunier's research on the sociology of colonialism affords another way of validating some of the stereotypes of Europeans encountered in oral literature.[39] According to him, Africans in the Moslem areas of West Africa reproach whites on civil grounds for excessive authoritarianism, stinginess and punctuality, and in Islamic ones for irreligiousness, indecency and ill-breeding. Devout Moslems accuse whites of being only half-hearted in their religion because it appears to be so inconsequential in their daily lives. They also regard as indecent the Western customs of keeping dogs as pets, allowing men and women to mix publicly and wearing tight-fitting clothing. Loud talking, speaking while eating, and urinating while standing instead of squatting are all signs of ill-breeding. Although elsewhere Western technology is admired as positive, Maunier claims that the West African Sudanese see it as the product of the whites' alliance with evil spirits.

The process of African self-assertion already detected in oral black superiority stories reached its fullest development in nationalistic political movements and contemporary African literature. In forty-four representative novels the most basic theme has been the humanity of Africans. Up until the mid 1960s it was defined primarily as a refutation of the dehumanisation experienced under colonialism. After that time, as novels started responding to post-independence disillusionment, the theme expanded itself into a more universal expression of man's disappointment, frustration and despair.

Novels set in pre-independent West Africa largely present stock types with the trader often identified as a Syrian, Lebanese or Greek shop owner who ranks considerably beneath the British or French on the colonial social scale. The most common characters are colonial officials, including district officers, commandants, prison directors, police chiefs and lesser bureaucrats; missionaries, both Protestant and Catholic; and teachers, ranging from elementary school through university instructors and administrators. Women appear far less frequently, usually as the wives of the men just mentioned or in a few cases as spinster educational or medical missionaries.

Colonial officials in novels written either by anglophone or francophone novelists typically exhibit the following characteristics: a sense of superiority, inability to speak the local language, aloofness from the colonised, and insensitivity to traditional culture.[40] In addition, a number of them are drawn as quick-tempered authoritarians who derive a sordid satisfaction from ordering or inflicting severe punishment upon Africans. A penchant for cruelty, not encountered in the oral literature, is present in a number of the novels. The officials who display the most tolerance towards Africans are the newcomers whose 'naive' idealism incurs the criticism of other colonialists. Didactic old coasters delight in recounting tales of their early days in the colonies to help these junior officers overcome their 'misconceptions' and understand the 'true' nature of Africans. While anglophone authors endow their officers with an obsession for acting as 'British gentlemen' in the tropics, the francophone ones provide theirs with a more mundane preoccupation with personal comfort, including sexual needs. In either case, however, colonial administrators strive to achieve a life style that is as British or French as importation and improvisation will allow.

Missionaries share the European supremacy of colonial officials, but tend to express it through greater paternalism towards Africans. Although they often speak the local language, in several novels they have not mastered its tones sufficiently to keep from pronouncing inadvertent obscenities in their sermons. Their overriding concern is with proselytism unless they are 'good' missionaries who show charity towards all, converted or not. Yet these positive characters seem ineffective and unable to counteract the bigotry of more intransigent clerics.

On the other hand, the hypocritical 'bad' missionaries perceive no inconsistency between preaching about Christian brotherhood and treating Africans as inferiors. Both Protestant and Catholic ones indulge in the strict punishment of sinners and servants, but only corrupt Catholic priests sleep with local women. Occasionally the missionary zeal with which they castigate polygamists and adulterers is portrayed as a suppressed sexual desire or perversion, especially in francophone novels. Several novelists have ridiculed the competition between Protestant and Catholic missionaries to convert the same people as a mockery of Christian love. Finally, almost all of the missionaries, whether depicted seriously or satirically, believe as another tenet of their faith that the African is a child who requires the supervision of Europeans.

Even though teachers receive no special exemption from the stereotypes of white racism and paternalism, they are often drawn with greater sympathy than either colonial administrators or missionaries. Considering the emphasis placed on literacy and education in oral literature, the respect accorded many educators in West African novels is not surprising. While school teachers and directors usually remain fairly aloof from their students, some of them insist that their African students equal European ones in intelligence and encourage the gifted ones to apply for overseas scholarships. Despite their formality, some teachers demonstrate a genuine fondness for their students by giving them friendly advice or board and room in order to help them further their education. The 'bad' teacher who abuses his students also exists. In an interesting reversal of the usual trend, anglophone novelists deal more satirically with teachers than do francophone ones, faulting them for brutality, pomposity, exploitation, hypocrisy and homosexuality. Often the worst teachers are also missionaries, as well, so it is possible that part of the criticism stems from the conventional image of 'bad' missionaries.

European women almost always appear as chronic complainers who make life difficult for both their servants and their husbands. Their insistence upon inspecting and rejecting the work done by their domestics is viewed by a number of authors as an authoritarian compensation for the boredom and frustration they experience in the colonies. Since time between furloughs weighs heavily on them, many spend their hours in gossiping, reading or writing letters. Adultery serves some as another way of dealing with the tedium of life, while others such as single missionaries or doctors sublimate sexual energies in their extreme dedication to their work. Interracial love affairs between African men and European women occur almost exclusively in the portions of novels that take place in

England or France. Some of these novels, especially those written since 1970, tend to discuss sex explicitly, characterising European women as either frigid or nymphomaniacal.

The image of Europeans offered by anglophone and francophone West African novelists is basically a sophisticated restatement of the stereotypes of white arrogance, aloofness and authoritarianism found in oral literature. While whites play more prominent roles in novels by French-speaking authors, works in both French and English fully exhibit the negative characteristics listed in the chart of African stereotypes of Europeans. The difference between the francophone and anglophone treatment of colonial administrators, missionaries, teachers and women becomes a question of intensity rather than content. Francophone writers portray them with greater resentment and more extreme satire than anglophone ones. Francophone novelists also rely less frequently than anglophone ones on pairing their characters—i.e. the 'good' missionary with the 'bad' one, the 'good' administrator with the 'bad' one. Bad colonists generally receive far more attention than good ones in anglophone novels, and European characters presented without a double are often drawn in such a manner that one or two positive qualities serve as faint praise.

The use of character pairs may be a way of conveying the ambivalence expressed in the oral literary portrait of Europeans. Although E. N. Obiechina argues that this device demonstrates a balanced attitude towards Europeans, the fact that the positive and negative attributes are presented as mutually incompatible and are incorporated into two separate characters remains rather damning.[41] Moreover, many of these good colonialists either are unable to combat white racism or their work is undone by their 'bad' successors. Europeans, therefore, really receive more criticism than praise in these novels, despite the allowance made for worthy intentions and virtues.

Francophone authors have registered their discontent with whites more emphatically than anglophone ones undoubtedly as a consequence of the differences between French and British colonialism. The policy of assimilation which declared the superiority of French culture forced the educated colonised to devalue their own culture. Only after they became *évolués* did they discover that to the coloniser 'black Frenchmen' were still only 'natives'. This deception was largely responsible for the hostility with which French-speaking writers protested against colonialism. In contrast, the British policy of leaving African traditions intact and utilising local chiefs whenever possible maintained white supremacy without negating African values. It had no vision of turning the colonised into 'black Britons', so it undermined only those aspects of African culture that impeded British colonial or economic policy.

Anglophone West African novels quite frequently include Irish, Scottish and American characters who embody the stereotypes the English have of these nationalities. For example, the Irish are shown as devout Catholics with volatile tempers, the Scots as industrious but stingy, and Americans as friendly but loud. In a survey that Jahoda conducted on nationality preferences in Ghana, he observed, 'the most striking aspect of the rankings is their close correspondence to those repeatedly found in American and British investigations.'[42] He attributed these correlations mainly to the importation of British attitudes via textbooks and teachers in the Ghanaian educational system. Generally the Americans and the Irish are treated more critically in anglophone West African novels than the English. While these depictions may represent an author's real sentiments, they may also serve as a mask for anti–British feeling. Since British ex–colonials enjoy considerable prestige at home, a writer who satirises them too much possibly risks jeopardising book sales by insulting readers in England. Cairns explains that francophone authors have less worry about offending the French, for ex–colonials often encounter unfavourable prejudice from their compatriots:

> There is a hostile stereotype of the colonial in France, recently revived by polemics about the war in Algeria. Tropical diseases such as malaria and amoebic dysentery are sometimes considered in a class with venereal diseases. With the possible exception of missionaries and, to a lesser extent, army officers, colonials are supposed to be ignorant, brutal, lecherous, lazy and very wealthy, often with a criminal record.[43]

Novels that include travel abroad reveal the British and French at home as more tolerant and understanding than the colonials in Africa. However, novels set in rural villages that describe Europeans mainly through hearsay rely almost exclusively upon the old stereotypes of whites as men of literacy, technology, power and cruelty. In such works the local curiosity about whites, clearly a mixture of awe and fear, increasingly displays resentment and ridicule as villagers comprehend the realities of colonialism.

The following chart lists African stereotypes of Europeans drawn from oral literature, public opinion and West African novels. The fact that most of these images arose during the colonial era probably ties them more closely to actual observation and experience than many of the European ones of Africans which predated colonialism as part of a pseudo-scientific theory of white supremacy. While many early white colonists came to Africa expecting black inferiority, it seems that Africans entered colonialism with relatively few preconceptions of whites or only the mixed image of them found in oral literature. Nonetheless, the statements in this chart remain exaggerations that were generally applied to all Europeans. More than anything else, they bear the imprint of colonialism, for in fixing an ambivalent image of his coloniser, the African may ultimately have created a divided image of himself.

AFRICAN STEREOTYPES OF EUROPEANS

EUROPEANS IN GENERAL

Physically, are:

1. peculiar, with long noses, straight hair, and they all look alike.
2. lacking in strength and virility, unable to work with their hands, unable to withstand the heat and sun

Mentally, are:

1. intelligent, literate, educated
2. technological, inventive, possessors of great magic

Morally, are:

1. arrogant, authoritarian, demanding, unwilling to learn the local language, insensitive to Africans and African traditions
2. disrespectful of Africans, think of them as animals, monkeys, children, inferiors
3. racist, exploitative, cruel, brutal
4. materialistic, rich, ungenerous, stingy, avaricious
5. lazy, concerned with comfort and ease
6. hypocritical, cunning cheaters
7. immoral, ill-bred, dependent on alcohol, sexually perverted, encourage prostitution, have no sense of propriety, demonstrate affection in public
8. unceremonial, irreligious (especially in Moslem areas)

9 unclean in personal habits, keepers of pet animals
10 honest, punctual, conscientious, well-mannered

Emotionally, are:

1 impatient, easily angered
2 aloof, anti-social
3 bored

EUROPEANS IN PARTICULAR

'*Good*' *administrators, missionaries and teachers* are:

1 concerned about Africans, fair, sincere, kind, understanding
2 often fluent in local language

European women are:

1 bossy, complainers
2 sexually frigid, or nymphomaniacal (only in recent novels)

NOTES

1. Georges Balandier, 'Les mythes politiques de colonisation et de décolonisation en Afrique', *Cahiers Internationaux de Sociologie*, vol. xxxiii (1962) p. 86.
2. Veronika Görög, 'L'origine de l'inégalité des races: Etude de trente-sept contes africains', *Cahier d'Etudes Africaines*, vol. viii, no. 30 (1967) p. 307; a paraphrase from H. Lelong, *Mes frères du Congo* (Alger, 1946) p. 45. Trans. is mine.
3. Görög, p. 307; a paraphrase from H. Trilles, *Proverbes légendes et contes fangs* (Neuchatel, 1905) pp. 105-9. Trans. is mine.
4. Georges Balandier, *The Sociology of Black Africa: Social Dynamics in Central Africa*, trans. by Douglas Garman (London: André Deutsch, 1970) p. 164.
5. T. O. Beidelman, 'A Kaguru Version of the Sons of Noah: A Study in the Inculcation of the Idea of Racial Superiority', *Cahiers d'Etudes Africaines*, vol. iii, no. 12 (1962) pp. 474-90.
6. Ibid., p. 477.
7. Görög, p. 297.
8. Livingstones, pp. 583-4.
9. Alfred Burdon Ellis, *The Tshi-Speaking Peoples of the Gold Coast of West Africa: their Religion, Manners, Customs, Laws, Language Etc.* (London: Chapman & Hall, Ltd., 1887) p. 339.
10. Georges Thomann, *Essai de manuel de la langue néouolé parlée dans la partie occidentale de la Côte d'Ivoire* (Paris: Ernest Leroux, Editeur, 1905) pp. 131-2. Trans. is mine.
11. Ruth Finnegan, *Limba Stories and Story-Telling* (Oxford: Clarendon Press, 1967) pp. 261-3.
12. Ibid., p. 262.

13. Ibid., pp. 262-3. All the brackets are hers.
14. Percy Amaury Talbot, *In the Shadow of the Bush* (London: Heinemann, 1912) p. 388.
15. W. H. Barker and Cecilia Sinclair, *West African Folk-Tales* (Nendeln, Liechtenstein: Kraus Reprint, 1970; first published in London: George G. Harrap & Co. 1917) pp. 22-3.
16. Heli Chatelain, *Folk-Tales of Angola: Fifty Tales, with Ki-mbundu Text, Literal English Translation, Introduction, and Notes* (New York: Negro Universities Press, 1969; first published 1894) pp. 243-5.
17. This story was told by Ojong Akpan of Mfamosing and appears in Talbot, pp. 389-93. This section comes from pp. 389-90. All subsequent page references will follow immediately in the text.
18. This story was told by Edwin Yorvor and appears in John N. Milbury-Steen, 'The Girl with the Jinn Lover on the 50th Floor and Other Stories: Tales from the Bandi' (unpublished manuscript, Indiana Univ., January 1974) pp. 546-9.
19. Robert Sutherland Rattray, *Ashanti Proverbs: The Primitive Ethics of a Savage People* (Oxford: Clarendon Press, 1914) pp. 143, 145.
20. C. A. Akrofi, *Twi Mmebusem: Twi Proverbs* (London: Macmillan & Co. Ltd., 1962) p. 128.
21. Rattray, pp. 143-4 for the first and last. The second one comes from Richard F. Burton, *Wit and Wisdom from West Africa: or A Book of Proverbial Philosophy, Idioms, Enigmas, and Laconisms* (New York: Negro Universities Press, 1969; first published in 1865) p. 67.
22. Burton, p. 67.
23. Rattray, pp. 143-4.
24. Burton, pp. 284, 304, 309; quoting from Bishop Samuel Crowther, *A Vocabulary of the Yoruba Language*(London: Seeleys, Fleet Street, 1852), no page numbers listed.
25. Ibid., p. 309
26. Bernth Lindfors and Oyekan Owomoyela, *Yoruba Proverbs: Translation and Annotation* (Athens, Ohio: Ohio Univ., Center of International Studies Papers in International Studies, Africa Series, No. 17, 1973) pp. 10, 62.
27. Ibid., p. 62.
28. Ibid., p. 10
29. A. H. M. Kirk-Greene, *Hausa Ba Dabo Ba Ne* (Ibadan: Oxford Univ. Press, 1966) p. 52.
30. Ibid., p. 83
31. Personal interview with Mr Bala Muhammad in Bloomington, Indiana on 26 June 1974. Mr Muhammad was a postgraduate in folklore and mass communications at Indiana University at the time. Mr Muhammad provided the translations and explanatory notes.
32. George Herzog, *Jabo Proverbs from Liberia: Maxims in the Life of a Native Tribe* (London: Oxford Univ. Press, 1936) p. 203; the second proverb comes from Finnegan, p. 338.
33. Herzog, p. 203.
34. Finnegan, p. 338.
35. Gustav Jahoda, *White Man: A Study of the Attitudes of Africans to Europeans in*

Ghana before Independence (London: Oxford Univ. Press, 1961) pp. 24–30, 39–42, 44–5, 48–51.
36. Ibid., pp. 54–6.
37. Ibid., p. 58
38. Ibid., p. 90
39. Maunier, pp. 84–5.
40. For a study of colonial officials in Francophone novels, see Mineke Schipper-de-Leeuw, *Le blanc vu d'Afrique: le blanc et l'occident au miroir du roman négro-africain de langue française* (Yaoundé: Editions CLE, 1973) pp. 37–64.
41. E. N. Obiechina, 'Perceptions of Colonialism in West African Literature', *Ufahamu*, vol. v, no. 1 (1974) pp. 61–2.
42. Gustav Jahoda, 'Nationality Preferences and National Stereotypes in Ghana before Independence, '*Journal of Social Psychology*, vol. 50 (1959) p. 170.
43. Cairns, p. 187.

7 Stereotypes Preserved: *Arrow of God; One Man, One Matchet; Houseboy;* and *Climbié*

While the four novels discussed in this chapter: *Arrow of God* (1964), *One Man, One Matchet* (1964), *Houseboy* (1956) and *Climbié* (1956) are far more recent than those analysed in Chapter 3, they demonstrate a similar but more subtle treatment of stereotypes. This difference in nuance seems to arise primarily from the pattern of ambivalence in the African image of Europeans, as well as the fact that they were written in the few years preceding and following independence.

Chinua Achebe, an Ibo from Eastern Nigeria, recaptures part of the history of his tribe, particularly its conflict with established colonial authority, in *Arrow of God*. All of the action of the novel occurs within the year 1921 during the transitional period from direct to indirect British colonial rule in Iboland. Achebe preserves African stereotypes of Europeans in his characterisation of District Officer Winterbottom, Assistant D. O. Clarke, and Wright, the Public Works supervisor of the Umuaro road project. Despite Douglas Killam's claim that the whites in *Arrow of God* 'are well-realised, especially Winterbottom', critics such as Eldred Jones, Gerald Moore and Charles Larson consider them little more than caricatures.[1]

This divergence of opinion appears to stem from Achebe's ironic use of complex techniques of characterisation to draw simple, essentially one-dimensional Europeans. In portraying Winterbottom and Clarke as complementary characters, he employs multiple viewpoints so that we see them through their own eyes, each other's, and the author's. Yet this device is suggestive of moon-gazing, for it merely reveals to us different phases of the same face. The traits of the whites remain the same; Achebe merely illuminates them with varying degrees of intensity.

Winterbottom's obsession with maintaining the highest code of British conduct in remote Okperi compels him to reprimand Wright. He regards Wright's weakness for local women as both an offensive degradation of the white man and an appalling lack of self-control:

> Captain Winterbottom had already had cause to talk to him [Wright] seriously about his behaviour, especially with native women. It was absolutely imperative, he told him, that every European in Nigeria, particularly those in such a lonely outpost as Okperi, should not lower themselves in the eyes of the natives. In such a place the District Officer was something of a school prefect, and Captain Winterbottom was determined to do his duty. He would go as far as barring Wright from the club unless he showed a marked change.[2]

Excluding Wright from the club, the nucleus of British culture for the five Englishmen at Okperi, shows the extent to which Winterbottom condemns Wright's actions as anti-social. This same preoccupation causes Winterbottom to dress formally for dinner every evening in spite of the heat. He regards self-discipline as the cardinal virtue of a colonialist, for 'Africa never spared those who did what they liked instead of what they had to do.' (p. 32).

European aloofness applies to all of the whites, since Achebe carefully depicts Government Hill as quite divorced from Ibo life. In this world which admits blacks only as servants, the English find the African climate hostile and Ibo culture alien. Even after fifteen years of service Winterbottom still considers Nigeria a land of strangeness with drums that tell of its primitiveness:

> After the first stretch of unrestful sleep he would lie awake, tossing about until he was caught in the distant throb of drums. He would wonder what unspeakable rites went on in the forests at night, or was it the heartbeat of the African darkness. (pp. 32–3)

The author skilfully exposes Winterbottom's insensitivity to African culture by contrasting his stereotypical view of it with the actuality of Ibo life and traditions. By first devoting sixteen pages to the causes of the Okperi war, then allowing Winterbottom to explain them to Clarke in one paragraph, Achebe highlights Winterbottom's misunderstanding of both the war and the Ibos:

> As I was saying, this war started because a man from Umuaro went to visit a friend in Okperi one fine morning and after he's had one or two gallons of palm wine—it's quite incredible how much of that dreadful stuff they can tuck away—anyhow, this man from Umuaro having drunk his friend's palm wine reached for his ikenga and split it in two. (p. 41)

Since Achebe has earlier described this encounter, we know that the only real fact in Winterbottom's account is the destruction of the *ikenga*—a carving of the individual spirit of a man and his ancestors. Akukalia, who journeyed to Okperi to deliver the message of war, refused all hospitality from Edo, so no drinking occurred. Insults were exchanged and when Akukalia, who was impotent, was called either accidentally or deliberately a 'castrated Bull', he attacked Edo (p. 26). Following this struggle, the Ibo say Ekwensu, the bringer of evil, stepped in and incited Akukalia to commit the supreme sacrilege of destroying Edo's *ikenga*. According to Carroll, what Winterbottom has failed to grasp is the religious value the Ibos attach to Ekwensu, for his secular explanation substitutes the influence of palm wine for that of Ekwensu.[3]

Winterbottom, nonetheless, prides himself on his knowledge of the 'natives' and frequently weaves Ibo words into his conversation to impress Europeans. He values the 'man on the spot' over the colonial bureaucrat in Lagos and newcomers like Clarke who are too modern for his tastes:

> 'I see you are one of the progressive ones. When you've been here as long as Allen was and understood the natives a little more you might modify some of your new theories. If you saw, as I did, a man buried alive up to his neck with a piece of roast yam on his head to attract vultures you might have second thoughts.' (p. 39)

The D.O. always cites this particular incident as proof of 'native savagery'.

Winterbottom's resistance to the directives from headquarters to accept the Lugardian method of Native Authority and to appoint Warrant Chiefs draws strength from his arrogance. He thoroughly opposes this new change in policy as 'stupid and futile', unrelated to the 'facts' he has gathered in the field (p. 63). Winterbottom confidently believes in white superiority as well as the deceitfulness, cruelty and tyranny of Africans.

Winterbottom's arrogance merges with anger when Ezeulu refuses to leave Umuaro. The enraged D.O. immediately signs a warrant for the arrest of the priest, instructing Clarke:

> 'As soon as he comes', he told Clarke, 'you are to lock him up in the guardroom. I do not wish to see him until after my return from Enugu. By that time he should have learnt good manners. I won't have my natives thinking they can treat the administration with contempt.' (p. 168)

Winterbottom's reaction reinforces the stock image of white authoritarianism, since Ezeulu's decision not to come to Okperi does not really constitute an infraction on the law. The D.O.'s expression 'my natives' betrays his paternalism.

Although Carroll points to Winterbottom as a European counterpart to Ezeulu, such a comparison has its dangers.[4] While both men display pride, stubbornness and authoritarianism, these traits function as personal qualities in Ezeulu but as stereotypes in Winterbottom. The similarities between the men remain those of a man and his shadow, not a man and his double.

Abiola Irele implies that Captain Winterbottom and Tony Clarke serve as complementary characters with the young man's sensitivity operating as a foil to the older one's insensitivity.[5] On several occasions Clarke's greater tolerance for Africans places Winterbottom's bigotry in bold relief, such as his remarks about George Allen's biased book, *The Pacification of the Primitive Tribes of the Lower Niger*:

> 'I found it most interesting. Perhaps Mr Allen is a trifle too dogmatic. One could even say a little smug.
>
> 'He doesn't allow, for instance, for there being something of value in native institutions. He might really be one of the missionary people.' (pp. 38–9)

Here Clarke's openness to Africa makes his relationship with Winterbottom fall into the syndrome of paired characters.

Later on, Clarke experiences a sense of disquietude when Wade, the prison director, removes an English florin from a roadside sacrifice on the pretext that he '. . . won't have the King of England dragged into a disgusting juju' (p. 182). Even though he says nothing, Clarke remains shocked and upset by Wade's sacrilege:

> This incident worried Clarke a great deal. He had convinced himself that he admired people like Wade and Wright who seemed to do an important job without taking themselves too seriously, who were always looking for the lighter side of things. But was this lack of feeling—for it certainly showed a monstrous lack of feeling to desecrate someone else's sacrifice—part of the temperament of looking for the lighter side of life? If so, would one not finally come down in favour of the seriousness (and its accompanying pomposity) of the Winterbottoms?
>
> Without making any conscious decision Clarke was preparing himself to assume the burden of the Administration in the event of Winterbottom's death. It would fall on him to defend his natives if need be from the thoughtless acts of white people like Wade. (p. 182)

As the new man on the field, Clarke has been seeking models to follow in shaping himself as a colonial officer. His idealism, however, seems greatly overshadowed by his lack of confidence, for Achebe portrays him primarily as an impressionable junior officer in the process of becoming a Winterbottom. His final thoughts about protecting 'his natives' illustrate the thoroughness with which he has absorbed Winterbottom's paternalism.

Clarke's sensitivity to 'his natives' remains more theoretical than practical. He concerns himself much more with his traumas about entertaining Winterbottom properly and arriving on time for dinner engagements than with the problems of the local people. Instead of demonstrating a real interest in the Africans around him, he shows only irritation towards his subordinates and anger towards Ezeulu. His treatment of the Ibos does not differ from Winterbottom's, since he also confirms the stereotypes of European arrogance and anger. Annoyed by Ezeulu's refusal to accept the Warrant Chieftancy, Clarke reflects the same authoritarianism as his superior:

> 'Well, are you accepting the offer or not?' Clarke glowed with the I–know–this–will–knock–you–over feeling of a benefactor.

'Tell the white man that Ezeulu will not be anybody's chief, except Ulu.'
'What!' shouted Clarke. 'Is the fellow mad?'
'I tink so sah,' said the interpreter.
'In that case he goes back to prison.' Clarke was now really angry. What cheek! A witch-doctor making a fool of the British Administration in public! (p. 196)

When he visits Umuaro on tour, he forgets to look into the complaints about Wright's mistreatment of his road workers. In writing up his report after his return, he dismisses the accusations as false, because he enjoys Wright's company and regards him as a good man. His failure to inquire into this matter betrays his actual insensitivity to the Ibos. In his treatment of Clarke, Achebe raises false expectations in the reader, for his initial liberalism remains unconfirmed in practice. At best he is but a partial foil to Winterbottom.

Achebe's handling of Mr Wright and his construction of the Umuaro–Okperi Road suggests a debunking of Rudbeck and his road in *Mister Johnson*. In an interview with Lewis Nkosi in Lagos two years before the publication of *Arrow of God*, Achebe acknowledged Joyce Cary's book as a provocative influence on his writing:

'... but I know around '51, '52, I was quite certain that I was going to try my hand at writing, and one of the things that set me thinking was Joyce Carey's [sic] novel set in Nigeria, *Mr. Johnson*, which was praised so much, and it was clear to me that this was a most superficial picture of—not only of the country, but even of the Nigerian character and so I thought if this was famous, then perhaps someone ought to try and look at this from the inside.'[6]

The similarities between Wright's and Rudbeck's problems seem too close to be purely fortuitous: in both cases the men run out of funds when they wish to complete construction before the rainy season. Wright, who considers decreasing the wages of his workers in order to expand his labor force, rejects the plan:

Mr Wright had then toyed with the idea of reducing the labourer's pay from threepence a day to something like twopence. But this would not have increased the labour force substantially; not even halving their pay would have achieved the desired result, even if Mr Wright could have found it in his heart to treat his men so meanly. In fact he had got very much attached to this gang and knew their leaders by name. Many of them were, of course, bone lazy and could only respond to severe handling. But once you got used to them they could to be quite amusing. They were as loyal as pet dogs and their ability to improvise songs was incredible. As soon as they were signed on the first day and told how much they would be paid they devised a work–song. Their leader sang: '*Lebula toro toro*' and all the others replied: 'A day', at the same time swinging their matchets or wielding their hoes. It was a most effective work–song and they sang it for many days:

> *Lebula toro toro*
> A day
> *Lebula toro toro*

And they sang it in English too! (pp. 87–8)

Wright's assessment of his men as 'quite amusing' echoes Rudbeck's explanation to Bulteel that Johnson 'keeps us all merry and bright'.[7] His observations about the loyalty of his men and their powers of improvisation may mock Johnson's relationship with Rudbeck and his poetic genius. It is also possible that Achebe is referring, however, to the prejudice of Rudbeck or that of Cary whom he has accused of misrepresenting Nigerians. The separate quotation of the work–song after it has been well described in the body of the paragraph suggests a parody of Cary's quotations of Johnson's songs, especially since it is followed by Wright's amazement that the men sometimes sing it in English.

Achebe has removed the romance from Cary's road building and has created in Wright a Rudbeck incapable of rising above his stereotypes of Africans. In what appears to be an attempt 'to set the record straight', Achebe concentrates on the unpleasant realities of colonial authoritarianism and forced labour. As a last resort to complete the project, Umuaro villagers are required to work without pay on the road. Although they see no logic in building a road between themselves and their enemies at Okperi, they have no alternative but to supply two work gangs.

When Wright spies Obika, Ezeulu's son, and his companion arriving late for work one morning, he becomes infuriated and stings Obika on the ear with his whip:

> He [Obika] made to pass Mr Wright who, unable to control his anger any more, lashed out violently with his whip. It flashed again and this time caught Obika around the ear, and stung him into fury. He dropped his matchet and hoe and charged. But Moses Unachukwu had thrown himself between the two men. At the same time Mr Wright's two assistants jumped in quickly and held Obika while he gave him half a dozen more lashes on his bare back. He did not struggle at all; he only shivered like the sacrificial ram which must take in silence the blows of funeral dancers before its throat is cut. (pp. 93–4)

The manner in which Obika submits to the public lashing further strengthens the image of white oppression, for Achebe has made his Ibos aware of the futility of struggling against European power. The analogy between Obika and the sacrificial ram seems to intimate that the Ibos themselves are being sacrificed on the altar of British colonialism.

Wright also exploits African women whom he uses as sex objects for the satisfaction of his own pleasure. Convinced that sleeping with black women helps white men survive in Africa, he analyses Winterbottom's problems as a failure to keep an African mistress. Even though Wright most openly takes advantage of the Ibos, his view of them does not differ significantly from that of Winterbottom or Clarke. They all see blacks as stereotypes rather than people.

Among the Ibos in the novel, the general image of the white man includes power, literacy and wealth. The power of Europeans, according to Moses Unachukwu, a converted Christian, is absolute:

> '. . . I can tell you that there is no escape from the white man. He has come. When suffering knocks at your door and you say there is no seat left for him, he tells you not to worry because he has brought his own stool. The white man is like that. Before any of you here was old enough to tie a cloth between the legs I saw with my own eyes what the white man did to Abame. Then I knew there was no escape. As daylight chases away darkness so will the white man drive away all our customs. (pp. 96–7)

His prophesy of cultural destruction conveys a sense of realism as well as fatalism.

Although Unachukwu identifies the source of white power as the Christian God, Ezeulu ascribes it to literacy:

'When I was in Okperi I saw a young white man [Clarke] who was able to write his book with the left hand. From his actions I could see that he had very little sense. But he had power; he could shout in my face; he could do what he liked. Why? Because he could write with his left hand.' (p. 213)

Both men are familiar with white authoritarianism, for Unachukwu refers to the results of the British punitive expedition against Abame, and Ezeulu to his own humiliating treatment in Okperi. One of the attractions of Christianity was the idea that it enabled converts to obtain the 'secret' of white power. The priest Ezeulu, confident in the superiority of his god Ulu, naturally seeks a secular explanation for European dominance. Observing literacy as the major difference between Europeans and Ibos, he understandably designates it the source of white power and urges his son Oduche to learn to write.

Although John Nwodika, Winterbottom's second steward, has little personal respect for Europeans, they have taught him the power of money. Without it, he claims, 'we have no share in the white man's office; we have no share anywhere' (p. 192). Working for Winterbottom has become the means of earning sufficient funds to open a tobacco shop.

Achebe in *Arrow of God* uses both European characterisation and Ibo comment to preserve African stereotypes of whites. By pointing to the failure of either group to understand the other completely, he skilfully draws what Wilfred Cartey calls separate worlds that touch but do not come together.[8] If we compare Achebe's masterful characterisation of Ezeulu with that of Winterbottom or any of the other whites, it becomes evident that he could have developed them more completely had he so desired. By choosing to paint them as one-dimensional figures, he has distanced his readers from his Europeans in much the same way they have distanced themselves from the Ibos in the novel.

Timothy Mofolorunso Aluko, a Yoruba civil engineer, places his novel *One Man, One Matchet* in Western Nigeria between the years 1947–9. The book reflects the history of that era by showing the appointment of Africans to Senior Service positions within the Colonial Civil Service, the rise of nationalistic politicians, and the policy of cutting down cocoa trees to control 'swollen shoot' disease.

In his portrayal of Jim Stanfield, the acting Resident, and Henry

Gregory, the Agricultural Officer, Aluko slightly modifies European stereotypes to form a 'good' and a 'bad' Englishman. He uses these two characters as foils to each other in much the same way as he opposes Akpan, a newly appointed black District Officer, against Benjamin Benjamin, a nationalistic demagogue. Counterbalancing these Englishmen seems to be more of an artistic necessity in the novel than an expression of ambivalence towards Europeans. Since Akpan supports the administration to the point that James Ngugi considers him 'a perfect example of the African elite whose self-appointed task is to make colonialism—lock, stock and barrel—work', totally distasteful British officials would detract from Akpan's credibility and render him a stooge.[9]

Stanfield is presented as a paternalist with a certain acceptance of Africans, including men like Benjamin Benjamin whom he attempts to understand:

> 'I must confess I've some sympathy for Benjamin Benjamin. It's quite a vision, you know, the vision of leading one's people. Don't you see what it means to him?'[10]

The question at the end shows the effort that Stanfield has made to take into account Benjamin's view of himself as well as the British view of him. His later assessment of Benjamin's past history admits mishandling by colonial officials, charging a British headmaster with needlessly expelling him from school and a British magistrate with vindictively sending him to prison for a libellous anti-colonial article.

He also pleads with Gregory to be tolerant of cocoa farmers no matter how reluctant they may be to co-operate with him:

> 'It's not enough, for instance, that you and I know what diseased trees must be removed today if they're not to bring death to the remainder tomorrow. We must let Momo's brother, the newspaper editor, the schoolmaster and the Salvation Army leader—all his precious lot of relations who can read and write, however imperfectly—know these facts. We must enlist the support and sympathy of these relatives of Momo to help us carry Momo with us. They're themselves only a little better than Momo in their understanding of the whys and wherefores of everyday things around them. But we must realise that the new race for Africa cannot be won without winning first the mind of

the African. Patience, sympathy and understanding—that's what we need'. (p. 13)

Stanfield's paternalism surfaces quite noticeably in his assumption that neither Chief Momo nor his relatives has a full grasp 'of the whys and wherefores of everyday things around them'. In drawing this general conclusion from the elderly Chief's reluctance to recognise the seriousness of 'swollen shoot' disease, he exposes his condescension towards Africans. Nonetheless, his intentions remain sincere and his commitment to the people of the district genuine.

He exhibits considerable sensitivity to Akpan and his frustrations at Ipaja. When a confidential government letter reaches him announcing new hope for 'swollen shoot', he regrets its blatant British chauvinism and worries about the impression it will make on the Africans in the Senior Service:

> At a time when Africans had started to come into the Administrative Service it was surely unwise to circulate such a letter. It was Government policy to appoint more and more Africans to senior posts and Africans, even of the calibre of Akpan, would resent the self–congratulatory tone of the letter. (p. 156)

Gregory, who also reads the letter, experiences no disquietude, since he only looks at matters from his own perspective. Later on, Akpan informs Stanfield that it is one of the reasons why he wishes to resign, 'I am of the opinion that if that letter is any indication to go by, there is no self–respecting African who would want to identify himself with the present set-up.' (pp. 165–6). Stanfield offers no rationalisation for the ethnocentrism of His Excellency's message.

Unlike many of his compatriots, Stanfield respects educated Africans as the leaders of the future. He looks upon Akpan as his protégé, confiding to him:

> ... his [Akpan's] appointment to succeed him in Ipaja was the fulfilment of the ambition of his career, that before retiring from the Service he would train and hand over to an able and honest African. (p. 23)

Stanfield's pride in Akpan's achievements in Ipaja makes him recommend the appointment of more Nigerians to the

Administrative Service. Even though shades of paternalism colour his praise of Akpan as 'a fine youg man who is a credit to his race, and indeed to any race', he does admire him (p. 156). In creating Stanfield, Aluko has modified the paternalism of Winterbottom who considers Africans as children into a liberalism that recognises them as adults. Beneath all of the Englishman's esteem for the men like Akpan, however, lies an implicit suggestion that such people stand out as exceptions rather than representatives of their race.

Henry Gregory, on the other hand, displays only impatience and arrogance towards Africans. Although much younger than Stanfield, his opinions of Nigerians reveal only bigotry. Quick to judge, he claims that Benjamin Benjamin is an 'over-dressed bastard' with 'nothing intelligent whatever about him' (p. 10). His intolerance also manifests itself in his belief that farmers who oppose the tree cutting policy should be imprisoned 'for standing in the way of progress. These bloody Africans need to be protected against themselves, and against their own ignorance.' (p. 9).

The Administration's directive that this matter be handled as democratically as possible through village meetings and information programmes strikes him as misguided:

> 'Ah, parliamentary democracy! You fellows in the Administration seem to forget that our parliamentary democracy has taken eight hundred years to evolve. Today the evolution continues. We came to their country only eighty years ago, and all the time we've been teaching them to stop killing one another or selling each other into slavery.' (p. 10)

Gregory basically seems to rebel against the idea that it is possible for an African to operate on the same level as an Englishman. Here he directs his anger at both Africans and the Colonial Administration, charging the former with backwardness and the latter with idealism.

Nunasu Amosu's claim that Aluko demonstrates an 'understanding of the psychological make-up of the British Colonial Administrative Officers' is unsubstantiated by the author's depiction of them as types rather than individuals.[11] Unlike Achebe's administrators who essentially reinforce the same stereotypes, Stanfield and Gregory embody different ones and thereby introduce an element of tension into the novel. Aluko ultimately presents Akpan, 'the Black White Man', as an alternative to both men, for he is the only administrator who fully endeavours to synthesise British and African ideals.

Ferdinand Oyono focuses on French colonial society in his satirical novel *Houseboy*. One of the most widely read francophone works, its sustained popularity in France is attributed by Macalister Cairns to its perpetuation of the negative image the French hold of colonialists.[12] Oyono, who worked as a 'boy' for a European priest for several years, has evidently drawn upon some of his personal experiences in creating Toundi, the main character of the novel.

Oyono preserves African stereotypes of Europeans in his treatment of his white characters, fixing each of them except Madame le Commandant in an unchanging set of 'European traits'.[13] All of them, even the seemingly liberal school director, Monsieur Salvain, are tainted by some form of racism. Although his variety of racism admits equality at an early age, 'young African children are just as intelligent as ours', his description of his former pupils in the school implies that older ones are intellectually inferior and only interested in sexual pursuits.[14] Salvain's heretical views provoke rather than dispel the bigoted opinions of his compatriots:

> The schoolmaster spoke with authority. He tried to explain African behaviour. Everybody told his own little African story to refute him and demonstrate that the African is a child or a fool ... (p. 61)

Toundi supplies a further illustration of white racism in his description of the entertainment M. Janopoulos arranges for the colonialists at his exclusively European club:

> M. Janopoulos doesn't like natives. He likes to set his huge Alsation on them. This causes a great stampede and amuses the ladies.
>
> Such amusement was provided today. The crowd of Africans who had come to watch the whites was denser than usual. Massed near the European Club we were beginning to infiltrate into the clump of essessongo trees, when M. Janopoulos indulged in his favourite sport. The usual stampede soon became a frenzied rout. The numbers of the sightseers had been doubled by the knowledge that the new Commandant was to be at the Club. At the first alarm I was jostled, then knocked down and trampled on. I could feel the Greek's dog at my heels. I shall never know how I

managed to get to my feet and to climb up to the top of the huge mango tree. There I took refuge. The Europeans were laughing and pointing up to the top of the tree where I was hiding. The Commandant was laughing as well. He had not recognised me. How could he recognise me? All Africans look the same to them. (p. 32)

The laughter of the whites and the Commandant's failure to recognise Toundi make it apparent that the whites in Dangan primarily think of Africans as 'large children' and regard black inferiority as a presupposition of colonial existence.

Oyono creates most of the Commandant's interactions with Toundi as examples of white authoritarianism. The Commandant, concerned with maintaining an image of dominance and strength, has Toundi go to mass with him one Sunday because he 'for some reason can't go anywhere without a native in the back of his pick-up van' (p. 38). He initiates Toundi by kicking him severely in the shins and by asking the Police Chief to raid Toundi's house in the African quarter during the night. The Commandant's discovery of his wife's adultery causes his abuse to become more frequent:

> The Commandant trod on my left hand. He was talking to Madame at the time and he went on talking as if he hadn't noticed. He managed to bring his foot down while I was off my guard giving his boots a final polish before he went out. (p. 118)

This passage underscores the Commandant's aggressive, sadistic personality. Toundi, perplexed by these arbitrary acts, notes on several occasions that they seem to satisfy the Commandant: 'he seemed pleased with his effort' (p. 27). The fact that the Commandant never fires Toundi, even though he comes openly to detest him suggests that he keeps the boy on mainly as a scapegoat and enjoys degrading him. The Commandant, however, does not succeed in frightening his boy, for Toundi's discovery that his boss is uncircumcised has shattered his belief in the superiority of 'the great chief'.

In drawing the Police Chief Gosier–d'Oiseau, Oyono combines white authoritarianism with cruelty. Gosier–d'Oiseau's midnight raid on the hut where Toundi lives with his sister and brother-in-law functions purely as a demonstration of white power. Later on in the novel this brutality becomes apparent in his method of dealing with his prisoner Toundi. The Police Chief who always carries a whip with him gives his African constable a lash across the back for not whipping Toundi hard enough. He issues the following orders for Toundi's second day in the police camp: 'nothing to eat ... Understand? You will bring him to my office in the afternoon. All day, the whip ... Understand?' (p. 131).

Gosier–d'Oiseau grants permission for the constable to take Toundi to the hospital after a blow from a rifle butt has caused a rib to puncture his lung, but only in order to preserve the prisoner for further interrogation by the Prison Director Monsieur Moreau. At midnight Moreau and a few other whites visit the hospital to make sure that Toundi has not died:

> At midnight I was pretending to be asleep. The Europeans came back by themselves. The doctor told the others what the African doctor had told him. I opened my eyes just enough to see. M. Moreau was there. He was swaying backwards and forwards on his feet. How happy he looked!
>
> 'He must have his punishment,' he said. 'Take care of him and send him to me. He's a dangerous element. I shall make him talk ... I shall set to work on him tomorrow.' (pp. 139–40)

Moreau, who during his affair with Madame had declared that prison was the place for Toundi, is excited by the prospect of torturing him.

Moreau's cruelty is made evident when he teaches two blacks accused of robbing M. Janopoulos 'how to behave':

> With the help of a constable he was giving them a flogging in front of M. Janopoulos. They were stripped to the waist and handcuffed. There was a rope round their necks, tied to the pole in the Flogging Yard, so that they couldn't turn their necks towards the blows.
>
> It was terrible. The hippopotamus–hide whip tore up their flesh. Every time they groaned it went through my bowels. M. Moreau with his hair down over his face and his shirt sleeves rolled up was setting about them so violently that I wondered, in agony of mind, if they would come out of it alive ...
>
> 'Confess, you thieves,' shouted M. Moreau. 'Give them the butt of your rifle, Ndjangoula.' (pp. 86–7)

Although Moreau approaches his task with such relentlessness that there can be little question about his sadism, Toundi removes all doubt when he observes that 'M. Moreau panted for breath' (p. 87), while Ndjangoula knocked the prisoners unconscious with his rifle butt. Moreau's enjoyment of violence far exceeds that of Gosier-d'Oiseau who generally seems satisfied with relegating the actual whipping to his subordinates. Unlike the Commandant who has to keep a black in the back of his pick-up van and kick Toundi in the shins to bolster his ego, Moreau has confidence in himself as a man of power, brutality and virility. Moreau, regarded by the Africans as the only white 'who is really a man among men' (p. 70), destroys whatever respect the Commandant has among the local people by cuckolding him. Moreau's conquest of Madame inflicts a special kind of psychological anguish on the Commandant, for Moreau seems to represent the kind of man he would most like to be—a man whose authority and masculinity go unchallenged.

The author builds the character Père Vandermayer entirely around the stereotype of white hypocrisy. More willing to preach than practice Christian principles in his dealing with Africans, he particularly distrusts 'natives' who take collection during the mass. Consequently, he searches Toundi after the mass to see if he has stolen any money:

> ... he made me come to his room. Then he undressed me and searched me. He made one of the catechists stay with me all through the day in case I had swallowed any of the coins. (p. 18)

Père Vandermayer puts Toundi under surveillance in case any coins are vomited or defecated. The zeal with which he chastises erring Christians suggests sexual perversion:

> He loves to beat the Christians who have committed adultery—native Christians of course ... He makes them undress in his office while he repeats in bad Ndjem, 'When you were kissing, weren't you ashamed before God?' (p. 19)

Père Vandermayer's shouting obscenities during a bout of malaria and his impatience with Africans cast him as the 'bad' missionary. His foil is Père Gilbert, the paternalistic but 'good' missionary whom Toundi extols as his 'benefactor'. Vandermayer's racism, more pronounced and less benign than Gilbert's, causes him to see

Toundi as a pest instead of a pet. Vandermayer welcomes only the Europeans before mass and ushers them to their segregated section of the church. More distanced from Africans than Père Gilbert, his sermons filled with unintentional Ndjem obscenities try to inculcate the precepts that his behaviour violates.

Wilfred Cartey has noted that Madame le Commandant is the only European whose racial attitudes change during the course of the novel.[15] When she first meets Toundi she offers him her hand, a gesture which brings a blush to the Commandant's face. On another occasion she asks Toundi about his family life and offers him friendly advice. She gradually becomes authoritarian, however, after the tedium of life in Dangan engulfs her and she begins her affair with M. Moreau. She acknowledges this change in herself as a loss of naïveté:

> 'And when people who really knew what they were talking about told me, I didn't believe them! . . . Well, there's going to be a change . . .'
> 'The prison–director knew what he was talking about when he said what you needed was the big stick', she went on. 'Well, that's what you're going to get, that's what you're going to get. We shall see who wins in the end!' (p. 85)

Her earlier handshake and conversation with Toundi were spontaneous; she simply had not yet learned the 'rules' of colonial society. Her adoption of a hypercritical attitude towards the servants marks her 'initiation' into the pattern of race relations endorsed by M. Moreau and the European community of Dangan. In drawing Madame, Oyono has combined the syndrome of the newcomer with the stock image of the bored and bossy white woman.

Madame's contempt for Toundi transforms itself into hatred when the doctor's wife convinces her that Toundi has informed all the 'natives' of her illicit affair. Both women fail to understand that as persons of privilege who require the colonised to perform all of their household tasks, they have automatically forfeited their privacy:

> In Dangan the European quarter and the African quarter are quite separate. But what goes on underneath those corrugated-iron roofs is known down to the smallest detail inside the mud-

walled huts. The eyes that live in the native location strip the whites naked. The whites on the other hand go about blind. There was not a soul unaware that the wife of the Commandant was deceiving her husband with M. Moreau the prison–director and our greatest terror. (p. 81)

Madame becomes embarrassed and infuriated by Toundi's bewilderment when he sweeps some 'little rubber bags' out from under her bed:

> When she saw me turning the little bags over and over with the end of the broom she sprang on me and tried to push them back under the bed with her foot. Instead she trod on one of them and a little liquid squirted out of it on to the floor.
> 'Get out', she screamed. 'Get out. You don't know what they are?' she went on, out of control. 'You don't know? Contraceptives: contraceptives. Go on, tell everybody. What a subject for all the houseboys in Dangan to talk about. Go on. Get out.' (p. 99)

In her eyes Toundi has not 'stayed in his place', but has become a judge—a projection of her own guilt about deceiving her husband. He has temporarily broken her myth of superiority, for she knows that his broom has swept too far.

Oyono depicts Europeans in *Houseboy* as persons of little imagination or talent who rely upon their skin colour to secure privileges in the colonies that would never be theirs in the Metropole. Thus, a person like Toundi who threatens even a fraction of their belief in white supremacy becomes 'a dangerous element' in their inflexible colonial world.

Bernard Dadié, a writer from the Ivory Coast, approaches Europeans with ambivalence, but still protests against colonialism in his autobiographical novel *Climbié*. Brench ascribes much of this phenomenon to Dadié's having lived longer under colonialism and become more psychologically involved and dependent upon Europeans.[16] Consequently, he tempers his protest by counterbalancing his 'good' and 'bad' colonialists.

Dadié uses this device in his treatment of the headmaster, nicknamed 'Gongohi', and his successor B . . . at the Ecole Primaire Supérieure of Bingerville. Gongohi as a result of his quick temper and heavy-handedness inspires fear but not respect among his students. A student finally challenges the headmaster's tyranny by seizing his wrists rather than submitting to undeserved blows. Gongohi, shocked and humiliated by this loss of face, almost immediately sails back to France. Dadié then praises B . . . the new headmaster, for transforming the school into a student–centred institution:

> By improving the menu and by giving the students a certain latitude, B . . . encouraged in them a liking for school life and for expressing themselves freely. The bullying also stopped.[17]

This is an example of a good colonialist counteracting the effects of a bad one.

Coming one after the other, Gongohi and B . . . technically prevent Dadié from making a generalisation about whites, since they establish the fact that Europeans differ from each other in attitude and behaviour. Although they may be modelled after specific individuals, they also suggest some of Dadié's conflicting thoughts about his Western education which led him both to knowledge and alienation. He describes this process as a subtle distancing from his roots, 'every day, slowly but surely, Climbié forgot his origins on a rice plantation, and the thrilling hunts for birds, insects, and butterflies. School assignments, his books, had supplanted the past' (p. 11).

On other occasions the scales weighing the good and bad colonialists are not so equally balanced and Dadié shows that the good colonialist is rare or ineffective. For example, he depicts the European headmaster of the elementary school in Grand Bassam as a conscientious but strict educator, who wishes that his school were large enough to accommodate all the children who want to attend school. The opening of school each year distresses him, since he must turn so many prospective pupils away:

> And the Headmaster helplessly watched the children leave, because the rule was there, inflexible. The rule is a barrier in the way of life, progress, and the impetuous existence of a society in full evolution. The Headmaster would have gladly enlarged the school with a single gesture. As he stood in the doorway with his outstretched hands straining against the door–frame, he seemed to test it. But the walls would not budge. (pp. 10–11)

Here Dadié simultaneously dispels stereotypes by pointing to the headmaster as sensitive to Africans and preserves them by noting that the insensitive colonial administration controls the funds alloted to his school and establishes the legal number of students he may enroll. The writer protests against the rigidity and authoritarianism of the government, which annuls the goodwill of the headmaster.

Even the author's most direct and sustained attack on the colonial administration bears some evidence of this duality. When Climbié, who helps politicise the local people, is arrested for having 'stirred up the peaceful farmers', (p. 140) he is taken before the most distasteful European in the novel:

> This twenty-year-old judge, in the name of the Law, undressed him, Climbié, who was nearing forty. And if he had protested or refused, this would have been 'contempt of court'. Everywhere, nothing but pitfalls. Is a prisoner still a man in the eyes of police power? For this judge behaved in identical fashion towards Climbié's friends who were naturalised citizens. Clearly, he was determined to make them understand that, unlike them, he was French by birth and not by decree . . . and, consequently, they also could be treated as 'objects' by a young man twenty years old, armed with the Law. (p. 144)

This Frenchman's misuse of his legal powers completely sustains the ideas of white domination and disrespect for blacks. Yet Dadié assures us almost immediately that not every white in the Ivory Coast exhibits the racism of this judge:

> Since the end of the war, some Europeans, their attitudes changed because they realise that their interests are tied to those of the natives, and that an era is completely over, have made visible efforts to smooth away difficulties and establish bridges between people. But are they heard? (p. 144)

Whether from a sense of fairness, ambivalence, or a fear of offending foreign readers, Dadié cannot allow the image of the young magistrate to stand unqualified. However, the author's use of the word 'some' and his question make it clear that these Europeans represent a minority opinion which seems to have little impact on the more widespread attitudes of white supremacy. These positive

Europeans function not so much to counterbalance negative ones as to accentuate them by damning them with faint exception.

A more subtle instance of protest occurs in the following description of European reactions to an African funeral procession in Grand Bassam:

> Always, a European motorist, hurrying to a business appointment, would cross in front of the crowd at full speed, as if suddenly he had the desire to behave badly, to dispense with manners, or to show off in front of other Europeans. Others, on the contrary, saluted and crossed themselves. The dead man had no colour any more. He was no longer of our world, once he had been relieved of his fears and his rebellious spirit. He was a lesson to all those walking behind him, for he placed the happy and the unhappy in their proper perspective. The dead man passed by the Europeans, and for a long time they remained there, saluting and thinking. Then they put their hats back on again and went their way, that is to say, with their dreams and illusions. Do they too think that life is only a dance before the final sleep? . . . (p. 42)

Here the 'bad' European who apparently wishes to impress other Europeans is outnumbered by the 'good' ones who bare their heads in respect for the dead. Although this may appear to be a compliment paid to the sensibilities of French colonialists, the phrase 'the dead man had no colour any more' seems to expose their racism, suggesting that only death enables them to see the African simply as a man. Dadié intimates that the African may win the coloniser's respect only posthumously.

A variation on this same theme can be found in Dadié's discussion of the attitudes of Europeans who enter an office and discover Africans instead of the French *patron*. While some whites turn around and walk out, declaring 'there is no one here', a very few politely inquire 'Sir, would you be so kind as to see if Mr So–and–so is here?' (p. 97). Even though he neither explicitly accuses all whites of rudeness nor credits all of them with politeness, he does point to the courteous ones as rare.

Even expressions of black and white brotherhood do not go without a certain ambivalence. The author relies upon a scene of French mothers with their baby carriages to establish the universality of mothers' wishes for their children:

> In the town–hall garden, men were playing bowls; women sat on benches, knitting, legs crossed, their prams near them. From time to time, they would lean over their babies, then sit up again, smiling. Like the black woman whose husband goes on strike, the European woman only wants her children to be well cared for, everything about them to glow with health, and no cloud ever to come to dull their eyes. Every woman would like to see her children live happily, and for as long as possible. Do not all mothers, the world over, think in the same way? Are not all hearts made of flesh, and capable of suffering, or understanding? Why suffocate these feelings out of selfishness? or out of vanity? (pp. 112–3)

Dadié endows this passage with an edge of social protest, for these bourgeois French women as a result of the inequities of colonialism face none of the hardships of African women whose husbands must strike for a living wage.

The most fully drawn white character in the novel is Monsieur Targe, a photographer in Dakar who has lived in the colonies for fifteen years. Without supplying the background of the friendship between Climbé and Targe, the author dramatises its growth. During a long conversation, Targe tries to modify some of Climbé's assumptions about colonists:

> 'Climb aboard that delivery–van. In two hours at the latest I must be off myself for Saint–Louis . . . We'll have a picnic on the way. I'll be with congenial friends. There's no standing on ceremony with them. Good men, very good, I should say.'
>
> 'Newcomers to the country?'
>
> 'No, no! People who have been here for years and years. And why do you ask that? So, are you all convinced that the old colonists are only loud mouths? Even among the new arrivals you talk about, there are some queer fish. It's a question of character'.
>
> 'And the influence of the climate?'
>
> 'That's bunk. We have moments of crisis. That happens to anybody. It happens to us in Europe, as it happens to you too, here. There are moments of blues, because, well . . . A man has his bad times. And he cries. But that passes. As for me, I've been in the colonies fifteen years, and just as I wouldn't tolerate some things in France, I don't tolerate them here, either. When a man leaves a place, he takes his character with him. I have African

friends; I call them by their first names because, for me, that's friendlier. I make no distinction between them and my European friends. You know that . . .' (pp. 115–6)

Targe acts as a kind of tutor, dispelling some of Climbié's preconceptions about Europeans. Unlike any of the other white characters, he has no external foil undercutting his liberalism. However, this does not mean that Dadié regards him without ambivalence, for there are the elements of a foil within himself. Targe's explanation of his use of 'tu' with his African friends as an expression of cordiality merits attention, since the coloniser traditionally used 'tu' with the 'natives' as a sign of white authority and superiority. It is noteworthy that Climbié never employs the familiar form when addressing Targe, perhaps from natural reserve or colonial conditioning. Later on in the conversation, Targe admits that few other Europeans share his opinions and acknowledges the difficulty of overcoming racial barriers in colonies, thus presenting Dadié's common figure of the 'good' colonialist outweighed by a large population of 'bad' ones.

During their dialogue Targe speaks idealistically of future brotherhood while Climbié emphasises present race relations. Targe, who has never been subjected to the political, economic and social discrimination that Climbié has known as a colonial subject, can easily overlook the present and predict a distant utopia. He is thereby rendered ineffective by his compulsion to dwell in the future.

Yet in spite of these liberal weaknesses, Targe broadens Climbié's understanding of Europeans and helps him to believe in the possibility of racial brotherhood. In ending the novel with a letter from Targe to Climbié, the author pays tribute to their solidarity and suggests that the future harmony of all races will eventually be brought about by men like themselves.

Although all of the authors in this chapter have depended upon stereotypes in their characterisation of Europeans, they have done so for varying reasons. Achebe has cast his administrators this way in order to emphasise the incompatibility between their world and that of the Ibos. Oyono builds his entire satire around stereotypes, depicting Toundi as a Candide whose naïveté is just as excessive as the authoritarianism of his whites. Aluko is required to have at least one positive administrator to prevent Akpan from becoming a puppet of the colonial government and one negative one to lend credence to nationalistic aspirations. Dadié's seeming inability to present a 'bad' European without a corrective 'good' one suggests that his involvement with whites as an *'assimilé'* was marked by psychological conflicts and cultural dispossession.

NOTES

1. Douglas Killam, 'Recent African Fiction', *The Bulletin of the Association for African Literature in English*, no. 2 (1966) p. 6.
  Eldred Jones, 'Achebe's Third Novel', *Journal of Commonwealth Literature*, no. 1 (Sept. 1965) p. 176.
  Gerald Moore, 'Achebe's New Novel', *Transition*, vol. 4, no. 14 (1964) p. 52.
  Charles Larson, *The Emergence of African Fiction* (Bloomington: Indiana Univ. Press, 1972) p. 153.
2. Chinua Achebe, *Arrow of God* (New York: Anchor Books, Doubleday & Co. Inc., 1969) p. 35. All subsequent page references will be to this edition and will appear immediately in the text.
3. David Carroll, *Chinua Achebe* (New York: Twayne Publishers, Inc., 1970) p. 100.
4. Ibid., pp. 94–103.
5. Abiola Irele, 'Chinua Achebe: The Tragic Conflict in his Novels', in *Introduction to African Literature: An Anthology of Critical Writing from 'Black Orpheus'*, ed. by Ulli Beier (Evanston, Ill.: Northwestern Univ. Press, 1967) p. 175.
6. Cosmo Pieterse and Dennis Duerden, eds., *African Writers Talking: A Collection of Radio Interviews* (New York: Africana Pub. Corp., 1972) p. 4.
7. Cary, *Mister Johnson*, p. 163.
8. Wilfred Cartey, *Whispers from a Continent: The Literature of Contemporary Black Africa* (New York: Vintage Books, Random House, 1969) p. 81.
9. James Ngugi, 'Satire in Nigeria', in *Protest & Conflict in African Literature*, ed. by Cosmo Pieterse & Donald Munro (New York: Africana Pub. Corp., 1969) p. 61.
10. T. M. Aluko, *One Man, One Matchet* (London: Heinemann Educational Books, Ltd., 1968) p. 10. All subsequent page references will be to this edition and will appear immediately in the text.
11. Nunasu Amosu, 'Review of *One Man, One Matchet*', *Black Orpheus*, no. 19 (March 1966) p. 61.
12. Cairns, p. 192.
13. While Hingot contends that these Europeans represent 'fairly accurate portrayals of the European in Africa', most critics are unanimous in their consideration of them as caricatures. See Georges–Louis Hingot, 'L'Univers colonial dans *Une vie de boy* de Ferdinand Oyono' (diss. Univ. of California at Los Angeles, 1973) p. ix.; A. C. Brench, *The Novelists' Inheritance in French Africa: Writers from Senegal to Cameroun* (London: Oxford Univ. Press, 1967) p. 53.; Monique and Simon Battestini, *Ferdinand Oyono: écrivain camerounais* (Paris: Fernand Nathan, Editeur, 1964) p. 55.
14. Ferdinand Oyono, *Houseboy*, trans. by John Reed (London: Heinemann Ed.

Books, 1974) p. 37. All subsequent page references will be to this edition and will follow immediately in the text.
15. Cartey, p. 63.
16. A. C. Brench, 'The Novelist's Background in French Colonial Africa', *African Forum*, vol. iii, no. 1 (Summer 1967) p. 36.
17. Bernard B. Dadié, *Climbié*, trans. by Karen D. Chapman (London: Heinemann Ed. Books, 1971) p. 64. All subsequent page references will be to this edition and will follow immediately in the text.

8 Stereotypes Contradicted: *The African* and *Ambiguous Adventure*

While a number of West African authors have deliberately preserved European stereotypes in their novels, relatively few have designed their works to dispel them. Two who have, however, are William Conton in *The African* (1960) and Cheikh Hamidou Kane in *Ambiguous Adventure* (1961).

Conton, a Gambian–born Sierra Leonean writer, briefly develops four English characters: two lorry drivers, Joe and Charlie, and a young couple, the Morrises, during Kamara's stay in Britain in *The African*. In each instance the overtures of friendship come first from these people whose warm response to the African student breaks the image of British aloofness, arrogance and colour prejudice. Conton ascribes the differences between the British at home and abroad to the insecurity the Briton feels overseas. To him the Briton in the colonies compensates for his anxieties about being in a white minority by trying 'to prove that he is superior to the Black man'.[1]

Joe, a jovial timber lorry driver, gives Kamara a lift when he hitchhikes to the Lake District for a vacation. After chatting on the road for a while, Joe invites him to 'have a bite and a cup o' tea with me chums and me' at a roadside cafe (p. 55). Although somewhat hesitant, Kamara enters the cafe where Joe introduces him as a friend rather than a hitchhiker, and overcomes his self-consciousness when Charlie gives him a hearty welcome:

> It was the first time I had found myself amongst a group of Britishers most of whom were meeting a man of my race for the first time. There was a brief, awkward pause. Then a big broad-shouldered man with a bronzed, weather-beaten face and watery eyes sitting opposite me broke the ice. He leaned across

the table, gripped my hand and shook it with a cordiality better befitting the reunion of long–lost friends. 'You're right welcome amongst us' he said. 'No better place than the Lakes for a holiday, no better way of travelling than hitch–hiking, and no better company to meet on the way than the present company assembled—although I say so meself.' (pp. 56–7)

Charlie, who has travelled widely, even to Songhai on a troop ship, sets the tone for Kamara's acceptance by the rest of the men. Throughout the scene it is Kamara, amazed at the ease with which this 'forthright, unsophisticated crowd' can relate to him, who exhibits reserve, formality and class–consciousness (p. 57). The hospitality that Joe and Charlie show him includes lunch, lodging and transportation but no obligation for reciprocation.

Mr and Mrs Morris meet Kamara while listening to a rehearsal of Bach's 'St. Matthew Passion'. Observing the depth to which the music moves him, they begin conversing and invite him to their home. Again Kamara's stiffness subsides when he understands the sincerity of their concern for him:

> On the way to the house I also received from the couple, and accepted, an invitation to supper. Over supper, I found once more how far the individual English couple at home can depart from the national norm of reserve and uncommunicativeness. This young married couple were deeply and genuinely interested in me and my story, and their interest evoked a ready response in me. (p. 90)

It remains quite possible that Kamara, who has earlier confessed to the reader that he does not particularly enjoy meeting people, may be stating indirectly that *he* is more open to the British at home than in public.

Conton draws Greta Hals, Kamara's South African sweetheart, as a refutation of the stereotype that all white South Africans are racists. Greta, who impresses Kamara with her straightforwardness, assures him that, 'there are many white South Africans who do not believe in *apartheid*, and I am one of them.' (p. 63) When he tells her of the contempt that black Pan–Africans have for her Prime Minister and their belief 'that the first war a United States of Africa would have to fight would be against the Union of South Africa', she scolds him:

'That's a terrible thing to say,' she said suddenly, almost explosively. 'Racial hatred is wicked, whoever shows it and against whomsoever it is directed'. She turned to face me squarely. 'My people are Boers. If they saw me talking to you now, even if they did not hear what I was saying, they would flog me. I have come to realise that they are hopelessly prejudiced in their opinions about the mental capacity and cultural achievement of your people—but that is because I have come to know many other African students in London University. But don't you see that the kind of thing you have just said only helps to convince my people that the two races cannot and ought not to live together?' (p. 64)

Greta appears to function as Conton's spokeswoman in this passage, teaching that there is no justice in any form of racial discrimination. In ascribing her change of attitude to her increased knowledge and acquaintance with black Africans, she summarises the author's method of ridding Kamara of many of the stereotypes of the British he acquired in Songhai. Her question prepares us for Kamara's change of heart at the end of the novel, for only then does he truly see the folly of countering hate with hate.

Acting upon her belief that familiarity minimises prejudice, she decides to introduce Kamara to her brother Jan and her fiancé Friedrik Hertog. Jan, a partial foil to Greta, has no difficulty accepting Kamara as a West African student, even if he later disapproves of him as his sister's lover. Friedrik, on the other hand, operates as a complete foil, for he immediately insults Kamara, '. . . I did not come six thousand miles to hobnob with niggers whom I kicked in the dust back at home,' and breaks off the engagement (p. 72).

Friedrik is prevented from being just a stock figure by Greta's explanation of the racial tension and violence on his father's farm that resulted in his father's death. Conton's dependence upon Greta's second-hand information illustrates his greater interest in narration than characterisation. By giving her the role of a social worker discussing the causes of Friedriks's bigotry, he loses the dramatic possibility of a self-revelation by Hertog.

While in theory Conton's interruptions represent only the thoughts of the narrator, in practice the narrative and authorial voices often appear to merge in *The African*. For example, Kamara switches from the voice of youth to that of maturity and/or the author when he halts his account of his voyage to England to attack the African equation of British reserve with racism:

> It is perhaps a pity that the British, with their traditional reserve, were the most successful of African imperial powers. For reserve shown toward a once–subject people is at once interpreted as prejudice. Two pairs of eyes meet across a ship's lounge or smoking room: a copy of *The Times* is promptly interposed across the line of vision by the Briton, and the African sucks his teeth and curses him in his heart. In fact, of course, the Briton would have made exactly the same gesture if his eyes had met almost any other strange ones. And so gestures create attitudes, and attitudes in turn give colour to gestures, and the waters are soon poisoned almost beyond cleansing. (p. 39)

Here the narrator essentially takes a bi–cultural view and corrects the false opinion of Africans by revealing British reserve as a cultural habit unrelated to racial prejudice. Yet the ambiguity of 'almost any other strange ones' may suggest that bias sometimes influences this reaction. 'Almost' in the last sentence, however, implies that the cycle of misinterpretation can be broken.

Kamara counters the exalted image of whites fostered in the colonies in his description of a street sweeper in Liverpool:

> We [Kamara and his fellow African students] did not lose respect for the white man—very far from it. What we did lose however (and long overdue was the loss), was an illusion created by the role the white man plays in Africa: that he is a kind of demigod whose hands must never get dirty, who must not be allowed to carry anything heavier than a portfolio or wield any implement heavier than a pen. Without realising it, we had come to think of the white man only in the role of missionary, civil servant, or senior business executive, one who was always behind the desk, never in front of it. We saw him as one who always gave orders, never took them, who could have any job he liked for the asking. So to realise that the man was perfectly happy working in that gutter (snatches of his melancholy whistling reached us faintly where we stood) was a most salutary experience. It was now possible for us to like the white man. For before you can like (as distinct from merely admiring or emulating), you must feel

kinship, a shared humanity, the possibility of common experiences and destinies. (p. 146)

The narrator gives a catalogue of the familiar stereotypes of white power, literacy, status and authority. Since the 'never' phrases are redundant, for a person who *always* does one thing logically would *never* do the opposite, their presence seems to betray a resentment of the coloniser as a man of privilege.

Conton not only uses Kamara's reflections to rectify the false impressions that Africans have of Europeans, but also those that Europeans have of Africans. Although Conton through Kamara often expounds upon the differences between African and Western attitudes towards marriage, family life, the elderly, and psychic powers, on some occasions he specifically addresses himself to European stereotypes of blacks. He refutes the idea of African laziness in the manner of a debater rebutting an argument:

> I have, since growing up, often heard foreigners say that my people are a lazy, indolent folk. Yet my earliest memories are of the incessant toiling of men and women in and around our dusty compounds throughout the shimmering day, cooking, sweeping, building, digging, planting, harvesting. There were few moments of relaxation for any grownup before the sun went down, and the long succession of babies which occupied my mother's snug, sweaty back was lulled to sleep by the rhythmic sound and movement which accompany the pounding of rice. There was, it is true, a well-worn hammock hanging from the veranda roof at the front of our hut; but we all knew only too well how thoroughly well earned was every swaying, creaking minute that our parents spent in it. (p. 1)

Throughout this passage Conton adopts a vividly descriptive style and an urgent tone, perhaps because he has been the victim of this stereotype. In *The African* he seldom integrates his didactic and artistic intentions as successfully as he does here, for he usually instructs as an essayist rather than a novelist. Most of his corrections of misconceptions operate as parenthetical remarks which could be removed without diminishing the unity of the novel.

Conton, who spends most of his energy dispelling stereotypes, tends to preserve them when depicting American missionaries. In their case the movement from appearance to reality becomes negative, for he exposes Miss Schwartz and Miss Costello as hypocrites. At first impressed with them, Kamara revises his opinions once he becomes their houseboy: 'Their conversation with each other and with us, their very smiles, as I came to realise before long, were artificial and assumed.' (p. 6).

The image of white hypocrisy grows even stronger when he reveals that they conveniently 'both received their call to convert African pagans soon after having been jilted, whilst still at high school, by a pair of young American pagans "back home" ' (p. 9). He discounts their missionary career as a compensation for spinsterhood, presenting them as straight–laced and sexually repressed females. Uninterested in the Africans and the African culture that surrounds them, their white 'superiority' causes them to lead extremely lonely lives. Conton satirises the tedium of colonial life in his account of a Scottish Assistant District Commissioner's success once in spiking their limeade.

In his handling of these women, Conton makes it appear that their insincerity and narrowness arise somewhat more from their nationality than their vocation. Although he portrays just three white colonials, the only ones he ridicules are the Americans. When Anderson, the Scottish administrator, re–enters the novel later on, Conton describes him as basically race–conscious but honest in his dealings with Africans. Even though Kamara remarks 'that the Britisher at home is an altogether different creature, and a much more lovable one, than the Britisher overseas', Conton never depicts an obnoxious Briton abroad (p. 46). It is possible that he uses his missionaries as a safety valve for resentments against colonialists, since they enable him to criticise whites without insulting his English audience. On the other hand, he may merely be expressing a personal bias or parodying the missionaries who supervised his primary education.

In spite of this one exception, Conton dedicates himself in *The African* to increasing racial understanding by contradicting stereotypes. He teaches primarily through comments and secondarily through characters that both Africans and Europeans must discard their false images and create true ones of each other. Although Ezekiel Mphahlele charges that Conton devotes so much time to this process that he lessens the effectiveness of the novel as a work of art, it must be remembered that didacticism dominates Conton's literary aesthetics.[2] As a result, *The African* exists not so much to tell a story as to teach a lesson.

The Senegalese novelist Cheikh Hamidou Kane subordinates social and political questions to philosophical ones in his novel *Ambiguous Adventure*. Winner of the Grand Prix littéraire d'Afrique Noire d'expression française in 1962, the novel basically presents the conflict between Islam and Western thought—which Kane has had to confront as an *assimilé*. Born in 1928 in the town of Matam in the highly Islamic region along the Senegal River, Kane attended a Koranic school for several years before entering a colonial primary school. After completing his secondary schooling in Senegal, he went to Paris where he earned a *licence* in philosophy and law at the University of Paris and a *brevet* at the Ecole Nationale de la France d'Outre–mer. He began writing *Ambiguous Adventure* in 1952 while he was still in Paris. Although the novel was soon finished, Brench speculates that Kane withheld it from publication until 1961 because he feared that it was not militant enough against the West to please Senegalese nationalists.[3]

Kane creates Paul and Jean Lacroix, Lucienne Martial, and her father Pastor Martial as characters that contradict African stereotypes of Europeans while representing specific aspects of Western culture. Instead of exhibiting racial prejudice and arrogance, they are thoughtful, sympathetic people who accept Samba Diallo as an equal, admiring both his mind and his faith. The author also approaches them as counterparts to his major Senegalese characters.

Kane portrays Paul Lacroix, the French administrator and parallel to the Knight (Samba's father), as deeply interested in and respectful of Africans. Although Lacroix is already quite conversant with the Islamic world view, he seeks to know it more fully. Whenever he addresses the Knight, his co–worker, he naturally employs the polite 'vous' form. His enrolment of his two children in the local school is also free from affectation, for his egalitarianism bears no traces of self–conscious liberalism. By moving in and out of the consciousness of each man, Kane offers us a picture of their inner lives, giving a sense of their human similarities and philosophical differences. The following passage functions literally as a demonstration of Lacroix's emotional sensitivity and symbolically as an illustration of his world view:

> At this moment Lacroix had to fight against the strong temptation to push the electric light switch which was within reach of his hand. He would have liked to scrutinize the

shadowed face of this motionless man who sat opposite him, and which he would have liked to relate to the expression of his face. But, No, he thought, if I turn on the light this man may stop talking. It is not to me that he is talking, it is to himself. He listened.⁴

Throughout the novel Kane establishes a polarity between the shadows (mystery) of Islam and brilliance (reason) of the West, invoking images of night *vs* light, of darkness *vs* dawn. However, he presents the light of the West as artificial, portraying Western intrusion in Africa as a dawn of 'cannon shots' and 'shining glass beads' (p. 48) and Lacroix's desire to dispel the darkness of Islam as his eagerness to switch on an electric light.⁵ Unlike the Knight who hopes for the end of the world as the revelation of all Truth, Lacroix believes in the truth of science and remains perplexed by what he calls:

> . . . this fascination of nothingness for those who have nothing. Their nothingness—they call it the absolute. They turn their backs to the light, but they look at the shadow fixedly. Is it that this man is not conscious of his poverty? (p. 78)

Since he sees the universe as purely material, he cannot really understand the African's lack of concern with the physical world. Even his name 'Lacroix' may be an ironic reference to his implied atheism or it may define him as a new crusader, carrying the gospel of Western materialism and rationalism to Africa.

Kane applies the same distinction he has made between these two men to their sons, Jean and Samba Diallo. Although these boys cannot comprehend the differences between Western and Islamic thought, they can experience them as barriers in their attempt to know each other. Jean, the only white in the school except for his sister Georgette, shows no intolerance towards Africans. He readily perceives Samba's special aura in the classroom, regarding it as 'the impression of a point where all noises were absorbed, where all rustling sounds were lost.' (p. 51). Jean's fascination with Samba and his desire to befriend him parallel Mr Lacroix's more abstract wish to know the Afro–Moslem world.

During an episode together Samba picks a flower and sadly observes that it is going to die. Jean's explanation, 'it is going to die because you plucked it', underlines his concept of causality (p. 57).

Samba, pointing to the flowers that have withered into seed pods, confuses Jean by saying, 'yes—and if I had not done that, look what would have happened to it.' (p. 57). Jean does not understand that Samba's preoccupation with mortality comes from his religion which views the universe as moving towards death and returning to God.[6] Nor can Jean, spellbound by the sight of Samba praying and weeping at twilight, fathom the cause of his friend's tears. Even though the splendid sunset and twilight enrapture Jean, his aesthetic experience is quite removed from Samba's mystical one.

Since Jean recognises kindred qualities in Samba, he finds the gap between his friend and himself particularly puzzling:

> That night, thinking of Samba Diallo, he was overcome by fear. But that happened very late, when everyone had retired and Jean was alone in his bed. That twilight's violence and splendor were not the cause of Samba Diallo's tears. Why had he wept? (p. 61)

Jean's thoughts about Samba Diallo seem to perturb him so much because they defy his powers of analysis. His fear may arise from his unconscious realisation of the incompatibility between his reason and Samba's faith.

The symmetry of the novel is so complete that Kane has synchronised the nine chapters in Part I (which takes place in Senegal) with the nine in Part II (which occurs mainly in France). Consequently, Lucienne Martial appears in Chapter 4 of Part II in much the same way that her Senegalese counterpart, the Most Royal Lady, appears in the fourth chapter of Part I. Lucienne who studies at the Sorbonne is Samba Diallo's closest French friend in Paris. A warm and intelligent person, Lucienne not only understands Samba's personal dilemma, but tries to save him from it by convincing him to join the Communist Party. Calin, who compares *Ambiguous Adventure* to a medieval romance, views Lucienne as a temptress who seeks to lure Samba from his quest for death into her pursuit of life.[7] It is Lucienne's devotion to life and her conviction that 'the possession of God ought not to cost man any of his chances', that establish her similarity to the Most Royal Lady (p. 117).

In the Diallobé country the Most Royal Lady advocates the need for change as a turning toward life:

> 'But I believe that the time has come to teach our sons to live. I

foresee that they will have to do with a world of the living, in which the values of death will be scoffed at and bankrupt.' (p. 27)

To her, Thierno is killing the life spirit in her nephew Samba Diallo, instilling in him a love of death that is inappropriate and unhealthy for a child. In Chapter 4 she publicly advises the Diallobés to send their children to the foreign school as an investment in modern life, even if it may mean the loss of some of their Diallobé values.

Lucienne correpondingly views Marxism as a way of curing both Samba and his people of 'that part of themselves which weighs them down,' of what she considers spiritual bondage (p. 141). Samba summarises and rejects her Marxist position:

'By your own avowal, you will consider your task completed when you have freed the last proletarian from his poverty and invested him with dignity again. You even say that your tools of action, become useless, will wither away, so that nothing stands between the naked body of man and liberty. As for me, I do not fight for liberty, but for God.' (pp. 140–1)

Her endeavours to persuade him to enlist in the Marxist struggle to free man reaffirms some of his faith and mysticism. While Lucienne's human qualities, especially her deep platonic love for Samba and her empathy with his anguish as an *assimilé*, contradict stock images of white women, it is obvious that she symbolises the materialistic metaphysics of Marxism. Her name itself is allegorical, since 'Lucienne' preserves Kane's association of light with the West and 'Martial' suggests the militance of her Marxist ideology.

Pastor Martial, who exhibits none of the hypocrisy or paternalism usually ascribed to white clerics, displays wisdom and soulsearching. The first chapters of Parts I and II set forth the similarities and differences between Thierno, the Koranic teacher, and Rev. Martial. Samba Diallo draws an explicit comparison between them when he first meets the Pastor:

Beneath a thick and greying thatch of hair gleamed the whiteness of a broad forehead which, in spite of the difference in color, reminded Samba Diallo of the forehead, with its skin hardened by long prostrations, of the teacher of the Diallobé. The long narrow nose overhung a grave, distressful mouth. In the dryness of the lips, their puckering at the moment of speaking,

Samba Diallo recognized the unfitness of this mouth for the utterance of futile words. (p. 110)

Even though Samba recognises in the Pastor some of the gravity of Thierno, the fact that Martial's forehead does not bear prayer callouses differentiates his faith from that of the teacher. Martial's 'robust, almost massive, body' (p. 110) contrasts with Thierno's, which has been 'emaciated, withered and shrunken by mortifications of the flesh' (p. 6), for Calvinistic Protestantism does not demand the asceticism of Islamic orthodoxy.

When Pastor Martial recounts the dream of his youth—going to Africa as an evangelistic missionary—it becomes clear that what has kept Martial from practising his faith with the all-consuming passion of Thierno is the West itself:

> 'It's an old story, all that.' The pastor spoke with a hint of melancholy. 'I dreamed of founding a mission in Africa, in some open countryside where no soldier, no doctor, good or bad, would have preceded me. We should have presented ourselves supplied only with the word of God. Our task being one of evangelisation, I should carefully have avoided taking anything in, even the least cumbersome and the most useful of medicaments. My wish was that the revelation of which we should have been the missionaries would owe nothing except to itself, and for us would be literally an imitation of Jesus Christ. For the rest, I was not waiting only for the edification of those who would be converted. I was counting, with the help of God, that the example of your faith would have revived our own, that the Negro church which we should have raised up would very quickly have taken over for us in the combat for the faith . . . When I unbosomed myself of this project to my superiors, they had no difficulty in enlightening me as to my naïveté.' (p. 115)

What Pastor Martial proposed to his superiors was a mission consecrated as completely to the work of the spirit as Thierno's Glowing Hearth. The refusal of the church authorities to accept it implies that matters of faith in the West are no longer free from the constraints of logic and practicality. Therefore, Pastor Martial's personal dilemma symbolises that of religion in a culture where science has eclipsed God.

The Pastor's wish that 'the example of your faith would have revived our own' expresses some of the hope for synthesis that subtly underlies the novel. Despite Samba Diallo's inability to reconcile the two systems, the Knight's vision of a new citadel built by men infused with both the science of things seen and the mystery of things unseen affirms Kane's belief in the potential harmony of Islam and the West.

Although in *The African* Conton relies upon authorial intrusion to refute misconceptions, Kane depends upon characterisation in *Ambiguous Adventure*. Neither author has sufficiently developed his white characters, however, since Conton, in elevating narration to the detriment of characterisation, prefers to tell rather than show and Kane, in concentrating on opposing world views, emphasises his Frenchmen more as philosophical symbols than as individuals.

NOTES

1. William Conton, *The African* (London: Heinemann Ed. Books Ltd., 1966) p. 47. All subsequent page references will be to this edition and will follow immediately in the text.
2. Ezekiel Mphahlele, *The African Image* (New York: Frederick A. Praeger, 1962) p. 22.
3. Brench, 'The Novelist's Background', p. 38.
4. Cheikh Hamidou Kane, *Ambiguous Adventure*, trans. by Katherine Woods (London: Heinemann Ed. Books, 1972) p. 79. All subsequent page references will be to this edition, and will follow immediately in the text.
5. William Calin, 'Between Two Worlds: The Quest for Death and Life in Cheikh Hamidou Kane's *L'Aventure ambiguë*', *Kentucky Romance Quarterly*, vol. xix, no.1 (1972) p. 93.
6. Monique and Simon Battestini, *Cheikh Hamidou Kane: écrivain sénégalais* (Paris: Fernand Nathan Editeur, 1964) p. 16.
7. Calin, p. 190

9 Stereotypes Transcended: *The Land's Lord* and *The Radiance of the King*

T. Obinkaram Echewa and Camara Laye have created Europeans who move beyond stereotypes and serve as major characters in their outstanding novels: *The Land's Lord* (1976) and *The Radiance of the King* (1954).

Echewa, an Ibo from Eastern Nigeria, pursued all of his university education and has spent most of his adulthood abroad. After being reared as a Catholic in Nigeria, he went to the United States to study chemistry at Notre Dame, followed by journalism and communication at the University of Pennsylvania and Columbia. His first novel, *The Land's Lord*, received the English-speaking Union of America Book Award in 1976 for '. . . a non-native speaker of English . . . who has published the best book of belles lettres in English'.[1] The first African to have won this prize, Echewa has been compared favourably by Charles R. Larson to both Achebe and Armah.[2]

The Land's Lord, set in a rural Ibo village in the early 1930s, centres around Father Anton Higler, an Alsatian Roman Catholic priest, and Philip, his Nigerian servant. Echewa sets Higler above the image of the 'good' missionary by focusing on his inner life to draw a fully developed psychological portrait of the priest. His struggle to feel confident in his faith is that of a unique individual coming to terms with man's relationship to God.

Father Higler's overwhelming difficulty on the mission field is that he remains a contemplative priest in spite of his decision to lead an active life. Having been protected for so long in the cloister from the frustrations of daily life, he contrasts his experience at St. Mary's to that in Africa as, 'getting a swimming lesson in a sterilised swimming pool and then being cast into a mire pit'.[3] The necessity of performing good works has ironically pushed him farther from God:

And thus it seemed that his own eternal fate had become
inextricably mingled with theirs, and he could save himself only
by saving them. In a monastery, the link with God was direct
through prayer; there were no measures of success, only of
constancy and fervence, and with practice the contemplative eye
turned the dim mirror of faith into a burning lens and fired the
imagination to a dazzling incandescence. But here they were the
mediators of his efforts, arbiters of his success, witnesses to his
failure—a saturnine jury between him and God—and he could
not be sure whether to blame his own shortcomings or their
obstinacy for their lack of zeal. (pp. 16–17)

The phrase 'the dim mirror of faith' suggests that Higler's basic
beliefs may not have been significantly stronger in the monastery;
they had simply never encountered sufficient resistance to throw
them into relief.

Within Father Higler's mind Europe becomes synonymous with
his monastic experience, while Africa represents life that is 'immediate, earthly and *real*' (p. 6, author's italics). Consequently, he
finds the God he brings the villagers strangely inappropriate and
alien in Africa. His God is a combination of the wrathful deity of the
Old Testament and the aloof one of eighteenth century deism,
judging but never encouraging him. The local epithet of 'Fada
Nwambee' (The Orphan Priest), given to Higler because of his
thinness, describes his relationship with this deity who appears to
have abandoned him.

Unable to trust completely in his faith or himself, Higler exhorts
his congregation to dwell in the peace of God which he has rarely
known himself: 'neither the contemplative life nor the journey to
Africa nor fervence in prayer procured peace in any large or lasting
measure.' (p. 112). The more thoughtful members of the village
detect the disparity between the priest's public answers and his
private doubts.

An examination of Higler's past reveals a consistent avoidance of
the active life. His relationship with Clare shortly before he joined
the French Army appears to have involved an unsatisfactory sexual
initiation, 'the promise of the imagination and the disappointments
of the flesh, shame.' (p. 69). While she is referred to as 'a girl of his
youth', she was slightly over twenty–five and Higler was about
twenty–seven when the incident occurred (p. 69). His remembrance of this event as the folly of an inexperienced youth masks the

fact that at the time he was really a man who had not yet come to terms with his sexuality. His broken pledge to return to Clare after the war demonstrates his reluctance to accept the physical and emotional demands of a probable marriage.

Higler, who enlisted in the French Army, abandoned it during the Battle of Verdun when his battalion was sent on a suicide mission against the Germans. In the course of this dangerous manoeuvre, his friend Le Roux was killed in a foxhole which Higler originally had dug for himself. It is noteworthy that Higler received his priestly calling precisely after his closest encounter with death. His vocation was not based on a belief that his life, unlike Le Roux's, had been spared for some special purpose, but on an instinctive desire for self-preservation: 'the promise to become a priest if he should ever get out alive.' (p. 98). He had intellectualised his fear as a covenant with God. It was only later during his first interview with Father Morris, the Spiritual Director of St. Mary's, that he acknowledged his action as desertion:

> 'Exactly when did you leave the army?'
> 'Three weeks ago.'
> Father Morris was startled. 'You mean the same time you had your vocation?' he asked.
> 'Yes'.
> 'You mean? – You mean, you mean you are a deserter?'
> 'Yes!' After that admission he had a feeling of sinking lower and lower towards the earth, and a craving for the earth to open up and swallow him. That had been the very first time he had admitted to anyone, including himself, that he had deserted from the army under fire. Before this he had thought of himself as striking a perfectly honourable deal with God. But after Father Morris had used that word, he had felt cowardice written all over him. (p. 35)

It was logical for him to seek admission into a contemplative order, for his temperament had long been ill-suited to the demands of the secular world.

Higler's decision to leave the monastic life and test his faith in what he calls 'a higher form of service', seems ultimately to be an attempt to exonerate himself from his guilt about his desertion (p. 98). His success as a missionary will serve as tangible proof that he has truly made himself respectable in the eyes of God and of men.

However, his inability to forgive himself, his preference for passivity, and his uncertainty of God's mercy undermine his influence as an evangelist. Even the church bell from England which he regards as his greatest accomplishment represents not so much his beneficence as that of friends back home. His good works lie more in his imagination than in reality: the partially constructed walls of the cathedral he hoped to raise in the village stand as a symbol of his unfulfilling ministry.

Father Higler's relationship with Philip demonstrates the process of dispelling a stereotype through increased understanding. The dynamics of this change have little to do with physical proximity, for after more than a year of benefiting from Philip's services in the chapel and in the kitchen, he still regards him almost exclusively as a 'good servant'. Although Higler begins paying more attention to Philip a third of the way through the novel, observations such as 'nor did he fail to note the strain on the servant's face all through the day', show a continued tendency to think of him only in terms of his function (p. 40). Even after Philip seeks Higler's advice about the murder verdict and the sacrifices to the Land, the priest's vision of Philip does not substantially alter:

> Thought of the servant would sometimes obtrude into his mind and so arrest it that he would stop whatever he was doing. He would wonder about the servant's plight. (p. 61)

The turning point in their relationship occurs after Philip recounts a humorous anecdote about his childhood. According to Higler, this moment of shared laughter gives 'a new dimension to the lacklustre servant, a human dimension.' (p. 94). From this time on, the priest feels a sense of empathy which culminates in a complete identification of himself with Philip after he learns of Philip's cowardice during the *Njoku* initiation:

> Father Higler now felt drawn even closer to Philip. For here in the middle of darkest Africa was a man whose life coincided with his own in the present, and in the future through their association as servant and master, and whose past also was a replica of his. Philip was no longer a faithful servant, but a brother. They were survivors of similar past hazards, co–expectants of similar futures. This meant that he was no longer alone; his life was no longer a solitary orphanage; he had found his twin, his dark reflection. For

in the secret heart of the taciturn servant was trapped an echo of his own life—cowardice, desertion under fire, abandonment of love. (p. 104)

Echewa's treatment of the phenomenon of overcoming stereotypes contrasts sharply with that of Cary in *Mister Johnson*. While Echewa explicates each step of the transformation, Cary relies upon a single incident, Rudbeck's execution of Johnson, to prove that the administrator finally sees his former clerk as his fellow man.

Although Higler may regard Philip as his 'twin', his analogy overlooks one crucial difference between them: Higler is passive but Philip is active. While both men face the same spiritual dilemma, Higler's struggle renders him unable to help himself or save Philip. When Philip comes to him for guidance about the sacrifices, Higler significantly advises him to do, 'Nothing, Philip. Nothing. Nothing need be done. There is nothing to do. Nothing *can* be done . . .' (p. 61, author's italics). He meets God's injustice with a sense of helplessness.

Philip, on the other hand, opts for action. Suffering from the tyranny of both the Land and the Christian God, he decides to confront and defy them because, 'at a point a man has to stop running and say to what is after him: Here I am! What about it?' (p. 28). His acts of blasphemy serve as his revenge against the gods, his refusal to be further victimised by them. It is in overcoming the gods that Philip becomes for a few exalted moments the Land's lord.

At the trial Father Higler's strong desire to save Philip rouses him from passivity, prompting him to cut Philip's bonds and urge him to escape. It must be noted that, unlike Philip, Higler's concept of taking a stand involves running. His actions ironically offer the servant physical liberation at the expense of the existential freedom he has just won. Philip's reaction of pushing Higler to the ground and grabbing his machete, however, save both his 'saviour' and himself. They protect the priest from assailants and provide Philip with the means of taking his own life—the last assertion of his new liberty.

Throughout *The Land's Lord* Ahamba, the senior elder of the village, acts as Higler's mentor, informing him about local beliefs, helping him participate in local life, and alerting him to Philip's plight. For example, he acquaints him with the Ibo awe of the Land:

'There is no escape. Not even in death are we free and disobliged. No, our union with it thickens even then. You know, when a child is delivered before it is washed and taken out to be shown, the afterbirth must first be buried in the soil. And four days later when the stalk of the umbilical cord falls off, we bury it also in the soil, and plant a young tree over it. The tree grows with the child . . . You see, there is no difference between us and the Land of our origin, no separation. If one of us has the misfortune to die in a foreign soil we send a delegation that may have to travel many days and nights to bring him back, so that he may be reunited . . . So I say to you, White Man, these people in your church now, they are like birds that have left their nests in a tree. They may fly all day long, but they must come back to the tree. Even you, White Man, are now of us. You did not start here, but you are here now. You have eaten the fruits of this Land; it has sunk its hooks in you. So even you cannot totally escape . . .' (pp. 61–2)

Here Ahamba serves as both a teacher and a prophet, helping Higler to understand some of Philip's anxiety about not offering sacrifices to the Land.

Ahamba spends a great deal of time discussing animism and Christianity with the White Man. He refutes Higler's contention that the Christian God is the only true one by pointing to beliefs as preferences, 'ah, my friend, beliefs are like wives, each man chooses as it pleases him.' (p. 63). He also emphasises the incongruity of 'The Orphan Priest's' evangelism, 'I am forced to laugh, White Man, because you think we are lost, and it is you, the wanderer among us, who must save us.' (p. 101). Ahamba detects the hollowness in Higler's declaration 'my faith in God, by God's own grace, remains unshakable.' (p. 63). He accuses the priest of being either untruthful or strange, and later opposes Higler's claim that this new church is one of hope with the observation, 'I have looked into your eyes and did not find them to be brimming with hope.' (p. 100).

The fact that Ahamba is the only character in the book who has come to terms with 'the secret which makes us human and keeps the gods divine to us', permits him to function as a priest to Higler (p. 145). The old man, who has successfully lived through spiritual problems similar to Higler's and Philip's, counsels the priest:

> 'Mine [my gods] drove me to the brink of madness in my youth. In age I have learned to buck their tyranny. And that, my friend, has been my conquest of despair, negotiating a new understanding with all these gods.' (p. 130)

The key to Ahamba's altered attitude towards the gods is his loss of fear. According to him, 'when our fears die down, our beliefs change.' (p. 63). Bargaining with his gods rather than being intimidated by them has brought Ahamba peace; he has demanded their cooperation and he has received it. In contrast to Higler who says, 'a god that can be understood is no god', but suffers because of his god's inscrutability, Ahamba sees no value in a god from whom nothing can be expected (p. 3). The old man's solution differs radically from Philip's, since it does not necessitate an act of existential freedom that places him above the gods. In daring to ask questions and require answers from his gods, he has not really denied their divinity; he has simply countered some of their obligations on him with a few of his own.

The last time Ahamba meets Higler in the novel is at the riverside after the priest who attempted suicide has just been rescued by some night fishermen. To this physical act of salvation Ahamba adds a spiritual one; he immerses Higler's head in the water three times, re–baptizing him in the name of the 'new understanding':

> 'You have now arrived. How many years are you? . . . This is not the end, though, only a halfway point, a stop in the middle of the road, though some mistake it for the final destination and never go beyond it. But you must go beyond it.' (p. 144)

He is encouraging his novice to live in an enlarged conception of both humanity and divinity.

The proof that Higler has accepted Ahamba's teachings becomes evident when he looks at the horizon on his way back to the village. It is then that the priest, who once castigated Philip for comparing the Christian cross to the jujus because 'some beliefs are superior to others' (p. 90) has a vision of a new synthesis: 'joining hands, sky and land were swaying to and fro like two dancers, humming: "We are gods together!"' (p. 145). Higler has finally achieved a sense of unity that embraces both Heaven and the Land.

Camara Laye, a Guinean author who lives in political exile in Dakar, places his novel *The Radiance of the King* outside colonial history in a purely fictional African setting. Often compared with Kafka's *The Castle*, Laye's novel centres around a white man named Clarence and his gradual understanding of African culture. Although Clarence's universe in *The Radiance of the King* illustrates a Kafkaesque lack of spatial and temporary certainty and a confusion of conscious and subconscious experience, his quest for the King ends in a positive resolution that Kafka rarely admits.[4] Laye himself draws the following distinction between his characters and Kafka's:

> My characters know better than I what this anguish, torment and despair are, but a moment always comes when they achieve happiness—when they attain it fully; while Kafka's characters attain happiness only partially or not at all and even when they think that they have achieved it, they have only done so temporarily.[5]

Camara Laye presents Clarence as a believable individual in the process of integrating himself into African society. While critics such as A. C. Brench and Charles Larson contend that Clarence is undergoing cultural assimilation, Austin Shelton convincingly argues that:

> The problem does not concern *assimilation*, for Clarence—like Africans caught in European culture—doesn't become something else, but by ridding himself of evils makes himself worthy of *charitable acceptance* by the African king. The whole affair, by turning the tables, is a protest against such concepts as that of assimilation in which one must give up one's own culture and blindly accept an alien culture. Laye is suggesting, rather, that although giving up error may be good, giving up one's culture for the sake of another is not.[6]

It becomes evident in the novel that Clarence is not a 'white African', but a Westerner working out his relationship with an African community by freeing himself of his ethnocentrism and egotism.

In adapting himself to African life, Clarence must rid himself of the inapplicable elements of his Westernisation. Laye handles this phenomenon both concretely and abstractly, for Clarence first abandons his clothing, and then, later, his sexual guilt. The beggar advises Clarence, who has no money, to settle his account with the innkeeper with part of his clothing, explaining, 'where we are going, it's not necessary to wear such complicated garments, and if you gave some of them up, you would at once be dressed in a style suited to the country you're in'.[7] The beggar explicitly views the stripping away of excess clothing as an adjustment to both the African climate and way of life. Later in a Kafkaesque court scene Clarence, still bound by Western taboos against nudity, balks at the idea of surrendering his shirt and trousers:

> 'Can you see me walking naked in the streets?' asked Clarence.
> 'There is no law against that' the judge declared . . . And besides, there is no question of your going naked. White men generally wear, I believe, a pair of pants under their trousers.' (p. 80)

Clarence significantly equates being seen in public in his underwear with nudity.

After he has lived in Aziana for a while, his attitudes towards public nakedness completely change:

> . . . but in the mornings, sitting in the early sunlight, he was no longer aware that he was naked. The air was so new, so fresh, so innocent! No, he never realised he was naked in the early sunlight, that cool, sweet air; nor did it enter his head to cover his nudity. The people in Aziana did not veil their nakedness any more than he did: they never thought about it; they just enjoyed life. Clarence was at that moment enjoying life too. (p. 167)

Clarence remarks on this same occasion that at night 'he was conscious of his nakedness', revealing his sense of sexual shame (p. 167). Despite his extreme breast and thigh fetish, Clarence has not yet accepted his sexuality. Imbued with a Western guilt complex about sex, he asks himself, 'how was it that he could at one and the same time abominate and yet so frantically lust after such a thing?' (p. 167). His thinking about his nightly exploits will remain ambivalent, until he has overcome his concept of sex as sin.

His experience with Dioki, the snake priestess, which Eustace Palmer interprets as a final cure of Clarence's 'lechery', seems instead to mark his initiation into the fusion of the physical with the spiritual.[8] During their meeting Clarence's ability to concentrate on

Dioki's face, rather than on her erogenous zones alone, indicates that he has lost some of his sexual compulsiveness:

> He could see her quite clearly. He could never see any woman's face, except in the oval frame of a hut window; but he could see Dioki's face perfectly clear. (p. 244)

When Clarence in disgust turns his eyes away from Dioki, who is writhing on the ground in a sexual orgy with her snakes, he sees a vision of the King setting forth on a journey. Although Clarence silences Nagoa and Noaga after they report to him and the blacksmith: ' "we saw the old woman coming towards you," said the boys. "She put her arms round your shoulders and pressed you against her," ' it appears that Clarence's vision occurred while he was having sexual intercourse with the old priestess (p. 251). Therefore, he has experienced a unity of his body and soul, or as Brench prefers, she is exorcising his sense of sexual shame while satisfying his desire.[9]

Most of Clarence's bewilderment about African society stems from his tendency to try to analyse experiences which fall outside his logical categories and must be intuited to be understood. The 'odour of the South' lulls him into a special state of mental rest and physical sensation:

> He was filled with an inexplicable heaviness. He was heavy with sleep; he was as it were drunk with sleep. His head and his limbs felt inexpressibly heavy.
>
> He leaned against the wall; he wanted to try to understand why he felt so heavy. But then he realised that he could not think even the simplest thoughts; it seemed almost too much to follow a single thought to its logical conclusion. (p. 146)

This scent which he attributes to the flowers placed near his bed each night in Aziana serves as a method of keeping him unaware of his employment. Clarence is still a sleepwalker, for until he comes to accept Aziana on its own communal terms, he will not be able to appreciate its unity and coherence. The 'odour' permits him to familiarise himself with some aspects of African life without the interference of his Cartesian logic.

In addition to giving up certain vestiges of Western culture, Clarence must also strip away his false ideas of Africans. This process begins in the novel when Clarence first encounters the beggar, his African 're-educator'. In response to Clarence's claim that he could fill 'a simple job of drummer boy', the beggar explains:

> 'That is not a simple occupation,' said the beggar. 'The drummers are drawn from a noble caste and their employment is hereditary. Even if you had been allowed to beat a drum, your drumming would have had no meaning. You have to know how . . . You see, you're a white man!' (p. 39)

The beggar has a talent for both informing Clarence about Africa and deflating his racial pride. In drawing attention to Clarence's whiteness, the beggar once again reminds Clarence of his status as an outsider.

Later on in the novel Diallo, the blacksmith, becomes Clarence's mentor in both matters of culture and faith. After Clarence interferes in the local administration of justice by halting the public whipping of the Master of Ceremonies of the Naba's Court, Diallo helps him see that not all cultures share the same concept of justice and that he must realise the full consequences of his intervention:

> 'Don't you understand that now everyone will look upon his backside with the greatest suspicion? It is only like feeling half the pain, to receive strokes the marks of which one can display to the public; but to have received them, felt them bite into one's flesh, and to have felt the flesh smart like fire, and then not be able to display one's weals is to suffer meaninglessly. In the end, no one will be satisfied—neither the people, nor the master of ceremonies himself'.
>
> 'You mean that, because of my intervention, people will feel that justice has not been done?' asked Clarence.
>
> 'Exactly. Why didn't you think of that earlier?' (p. 214)

What to Clarence was an act of kindness in Western terms has caused psychological pain in this culture. A similar point is made when Diallo, hearing about horse-shoes for the first time, regards them as a cruel practice:

> 'I couldn't bring myself to do a thing like that,' said Diallo. 'I wouldn't have the heart.'
>
> 'Well, it was quite a different song when you were watching the

backside of the master of ceremonies!' said Clarence.
'Is that any reason why you should accuse me of being lacking in sensitivity?' asked Diallo. He gazed thoughtfully at Clarence.
'They told me,' he went on, 'that you refused to spit upon the master of ceremonies' bottom.'
'But how could I do such a thing?' cried Clarence.
'I don't think you understand what I mean.'
'I understand you perfectly. Noaga explained it to me.'
'Well, then?'
'I just couldn't. I'm too sensitive.' (p. 213)

Diallo makes it clear that ideas of sensitivity are just as relativistic as those of justice. In Aziana the custom of spitting on the posterior of the guilty person is a way of giving him some relief from the burning sensation of the caning. While Clarence may ascribe his refusal to follow this custom to his 'sensitivity', the local people see it as a sign of his callousness.

Finally Clarence must free himself of his sense of racial superiority. When the beggar tells Clarence that the King does not receive just anyone, Clarence expresses his white arrogance, ' "I am not 'just anybody'," replied Clarence. "I am a white man." ' (p. 10). During the incident of the stolen coat, Clarence feels most embarrassed when he passes a group of white men. Their complete disrespect for him is especially devastating, since it makes him aware of his outcast state and robs him of the self–importance he derives from being white. In the black world he can take pride in being white; in the white world he can take pride in nothing.

This experience seems to have inscribed itself so indelibly on his subconscious mind that much of his behaviour in Aziana may be seen as an effort to preserve his self–esteem even at the cost of self–delusion. After Clarence confesses to Diallo that he has not always waited for the King as he should have, he reflects:

> He thought that the odour, the South . . . Yes, they existed, without doubt, the odour, and the South. But had there been nothing else . . . Oh! if there had only been the odour and the South, if there had not been the secret complaisance, that secret complicity! . . . (p. 255)

According to J. M. Ita, what Clarence is ashamed of in this passage is not having fathered all of the half–caste children in the village, but having 'pretended not to know in order to preserve a false semblance of dignity'.[10] The Master of Ceremonies who apparently functions as Clarence's conscience also emphasises Clarence's self-deceit:

> 'Have you the effrontery to tell me that you didn't know about that either? There's a lot of things you know nothing about! Perhaps there are one or two things that you really don't know anything about, but there are too many things that you simply pretend not to know anything about.' (p. 267)

This paragraph echoes his words on an earlier occasion which Clarence dismissed as a dream:

> 'What's your little game? . . . You're not silly, Clarence. You know quite well the difference between Akissi and the women of the harem who visit you during the night . . . Come on, admit it! Stop putting on this act which deceives no one! . . . What else can you do now but confess? . . . All those little half-caste brats in the courtyard of the harem didn't just drop from the clouds!' (p. 200)

Ita attributes Clarence's self-deception to his pride, which cannot accept the indignity of having been sold to the Naba and of having been given the only job in Aziana that requires no special training or hereditary qualification.[11] Since Clarence thinks he should do something more prestigious because he is white, he does not wish to admit that he is really 'just anybody'. The Master of Ceremonies on the day of the King's arrival finally exposes all of the things that Clarence has tried to hide from himself. This confrontation between the two men, unlike the earlier repressed one, acts as Clarence's moment of self-realisation and marks the beginning of his true humility.

Once he discards his white pride, he is able to see himself as a man like everyone else, whose only gift is his good-will. Clarence, who now has a true image of himself that admits both his baseness and his goodness, is ready for his salvation:

> 'Did you not know that I was waiting for you?' asked the king.
> And Clarence placed his lips upon the faint and yet tremendous beating of that heart. Then the king slowly closed his arms

around him, and his great mantle swept around him, and enveloped him for ever. (p. 284)

During all of his years of stripping away false images of culture, of others, and of himself, Clarence has faithfully awaited the King. The King, whether interpreted as a God–figure or, as Harold Scheub suggests, the best part of the self, receives Clarence in an act which Diallo calls 'pity' but others would call grace.[12] In this moment the symbolism of Clarence expands; Clarence, the individual and the Westerner, is now everyman.[13]

In transcending stereotypes of Europeans, both Echewa and Laye have created white characters who move from a sense of isolation and Western superiority to one of brotherhood. Echewa permits Higler, however, to operate as a self–aware individual conscious of the complexity of himself and of the human spiritual dilemma. Unlike Clarence, Higler finds a new communion with men rather than a complete one with the King, for in Echewa's universe man can come to terms but can never efface the conflict between humanity and divinity. Clarence's effort in *The Radiance of the King* to integrate himself into the life of Aziana becomes the quest of all men who seek redemption through humility and faith.

NOTES

1. English-speaking Union of America as quoted in John Updike, 'African Accents', *New Yorker* (16 May 1977), p. 146.
2. *African Panorama*, interview with Charles R. Larson by Lee Nichols, prod. Voice of America Staff. Tape made available to me by VOA for private listening on 25 January 1978, in Falmer, England.
3. T. Obinkaram Echewa, *The Land's Lord* (London: Heinemann Ed. Books Ltd., 1976) p. 49. All subsequent page references will be to this edition, and will follow immediately in the text.
4. For a full-length study of the Kafkaesque elements in *The Radiance of the King*, see Patricia Anne Deduck, 'Franz Kafka's Influence on Camara Laye's *Le Regard du Roi* (thesis, Indiana Univ., 1970); and J. M. Ita, 'Laye's *Radiance of the King* and Kafka's *Castle*', *Odu*, n.s., No. 4 (Oct. 1970) pp. 18–45.
5. Camara Laye, 'Kafka et moi', in *Camara Laye: écrivain guinéen* by Monique and Simon Battestini (Paris: Fernand Nathan, Editeur, 1964) p. 37. Trans. is mine.
6. A. C. Brench, *The Novelists' Inheritance in French Africa: Writers from Senegal to Cameroon* (London: Oxford Univ. Press, 1967) p. 121; Larson, p. 174; Austin J. Shelton, 'Cultural Reversal as a Motif of Protest by Laye and Dadié', *L'Esprit créateur*, vol. x, no. 3 (Fall 1970) p. 216.
7. Camara Laye, *The Radiance of the King*, trans. by James Kirkup (Glasgow: Fontana/Collins, 1975) p. 63. All subsequent page references will be to this

edition, and will follow immediately in the text.
8. Eustace Palmer, *An Introduction to the African Novel* (New York: Africana Pub. Corp., 1972) p. 112.
9. A. C. Brench, 'Camara Laye: Idealist & Mystic', *African Literature Today*, No. 2 (January 1969) p. 23.
10. Ita, p. 37.
11. Ibid., pp. 33-4.
12. Harold Scheub, 'Symbolism in Camara Laye's *Le Regard du Roi*', *Ba Shiru*, vol. i, no. 1 (Spring 1970) p. 35.
13. Larson, p. 226.

Conclusion

It cannot be said that the crucial indicator of a novelist's sensitivity to a cross-cultural situation naturally lies in the image he presents of members of the *other* culture. Although some authors, such as Southon and Joseph, perpetuate racist stereotypes for ethnocentric reasons, many elect to use them for artistic ones. In such instances stock images may function as they do in Achebe's novel as a distancing device to underline the alienation between the coloniser and the colonised, or they may be invoked as symbols that serve a literary rather than a racist purpose as in the case of Greene, or they may be employed in the style of Oyono as a means of satire. It is only when stereotypes are expressions of an author's sense of racial or cultural superiority that art has been sacrificed to propaganda and the novel suffers. Partially as a consequence of the ambivalence of the African image of Europeans and the later historical period in which West Africans are writing, novelists like Achebe, Oyono, Aluko, and Dadié have preserved stereotypes in a more sophisticated manner than their European counterparts.

Novels which contradict stereotypes appear to be the most awkward to write, for their authors, reacting against stock images, are prone to become overly didactic. Even though such writers usually depend upon characterisation and digression, Delavignette has experimented with multiple points of view to dispel stereotypes. This type of novel often deteriorates because of either too much authorial intrusion and anthropological explanation or insufficient character development.

Novels which transcend stereotypes are among the least dated and most lasting works that portray the interaction of Africans and Europeans in West Africa. Written almost exclusively by professional writers with a talent for characterisation, such novels are peopled by believable Africans or Europeans who operate as individuals. With the exception of Cary who draws a largely external portrait of Mister Johnson, most authors of these works approach their characters psychologically, emphasising both their inner and outer lives. Laye, in addition, accentuates Clarence's spiritual progress, depicting him as both a man and a pilgrim. The novelists who move beyond stereotypes ultimately stand alone as the only authors that develop their Africans and Europeans as unique persons.

Bibliography

BRITISH

Adams, W. H.	*The Dominant Race* London: Smith, Elder & Co., 1913.
Brook, Ian	*Jimmy Riddle* New York: G. P. Putnam's Sons, 1961.
Broome, Adam	*The Porro Palaver* London: Geoffrey Bles, 1929.
Cary, Joyce	*The African Witch* London: Michael Joseph, 1959.
	Aissa Saved London: Michael Joseph, 1959.
	An American Visitor New York: Harper & Brothers, Publishers, 1961.
	Castle Corner London: Michael Joseph, 1952.
	Mister Johnson New York: Berkley Publishing Corp., 1964.
Courlander, Harold	*The African* New York: Crown Publishers, Inc., 1969.
Davidson, Basil	*The Rapids* London: Jonathan Cape, 1956.
Dawson, A. J.	*African Nights Entertainment* New York: Dodd, Mead & Co., 1900.
Greene, Graham	*The Heart of the Matter* New York: Viking Press, 1971.
Hastings, A. C. G.	*Gone Native* New York: Macaulay Co., 1929.
Holtby, Winifred	*Mandoa, Mandoa! A Comedy of Irrelevance* London: Collins, 1933.
Hutchinson, Ray Coryton	*The Answering Glory* New York: Farrar London: Collins, 1933.

Johnston, Harry	*The Gay-Dombeys* New York: Macmillan Co., 1920.
	The History of a Slave London: Kegan Paul, Tench & Co., 1889.
	The Man Who Did the Right Thing New York: The Macmillan Co., 1921.
Loader, W. R.	*The Guinea Stamp* London: Jonathan Cape, 1956.
	No Joy in Africa London: Jonathan Cape, 1955.
Perham, Margery Freda	*Major Dane's Garden* London: Hutchinson & Co., 1925.
Rattray, R. S.	*The Leopard Priestess* New York: D. Appleton–Century Co., 1935.
Southon, Arthur Eustace	*A Yellow Napoleon: A Romance of West Africa* Freeport, New York: Books for Libraries Press, 1972.
Steen, Marguerite	*The Sun is My Undoing* New York: The Viking Press, 1941.
Warner, Esther S.	*The Silk-Cotton Tree* London: Victor Gollancz, Ltd., 1958.

FRENCH

Binger, Louis–Gustave	*Le serment de l'explorateur* Paris: Ernest Flammarion, Editeur, 1904.
Charbonneau, Louis	*Fièvres d'Afrique* Paris: J. Ferenczi et Fils, 1926.
	Mambu et son amour Paris: René Kieffer, 1925.
Chaumel, Alfred	*Aminata, femme noire* Paris: Les Presses françaises, 1923.
Conchon, Georges	*L'état sauvage* Paris: Editions Albin Michel, 1964.
Crouzat, Henri	*Azizah de Niamkoko* Paris: Presses Cité, 1958.
Delavignette, Robert Louis	*Les Paysans noir: récit soudanais en douze mois* Paris: Librairie Stock, 1931.
Demaison, André	*La comédie des animaux* Paris: Flammarion, 1956.
	Diato: roman de l'homme noir qui eut trois

	femmes en mourut Paris: Albin Michel, 1923.
	Le jugement des ténèbres Paris: Editions Bernard Grasset, 1935.
Diole, Philippe	*Okapi Fever*, trans. Peter Green. London: Souvenir Press, Ltd., 1965.
Dornin, Pierre	*Ames soudanaises* Paris: Société d'Editions Littéraires et Artistiques, 1906.
Faivre, Louis (pseud. of Robert Louis Delavignette)	*Toum* Paris: Bernard Grasset, 1926.
Garnier, Christine	*Va-t'en avec les tiens!* Paris: Bernard Grasset, 1951.
Gary, Romain	*Les racines du ciel* Paris: Gallimard, 1956.
Joseph, Gaston	*Koffi: roman vrai d'un noir* Paris: Editions du Monde Nouveau, 1922.
Larteguy, Jean	*The Hounds of Hell*, trans. Ian Fielding. London: Cassell, 1966.
Leblond, Marius and Ary	*Ulysse, Cafre ou l'histoire dorée d'un noir* Paris: Les Editions de France, 1924.
Loti, Pierre	*Le roman d'un spahi.* Paris: Calmann-Lévy, n.d.
Maran, René	*Batouala* Monte Carlo: Les Editions de l'Imprimerie Nationale de Monaco, 1938.
	Djouma, chien de brousse. Paris: Albin Michel, 1927.
Mégret, Christian	*Les anthropophages* Paris: Arthème Fayard et Cie, 1937.
Mille, Pierre	*Sur la vaste terre* Paris: Calmann-Lévy, 1905.
Pilotaz, Paul	*Man Alone*, trans. J. H. F. McEwen. New York: Roy Publishers, 1952.
Randau, Robert (pseud. of Robert Arnaud)	*Le chef des porte-plume* Paris: Editions du Monde Nouveau, 1922.
	Les terrasses de Tombouctou Paris: Edition du Livre Mensuel, 1920.
Roussel, Raymond	*Impressions d'Afrique* Paris: Jean-Jacques Pauvert, 1963.

Tharaud, Jerome and Jean	*La randonnée de Samba Diouf* Paris: Librairie Plon, 1922.

ANGLOPHONE AFRICAN

Achebe, Chinua	*Arrow of God* New York: Anchor Books, Doubleday & Co., 1969. *No Longer at Ease* New York: Astor-Honor, Inc., 1961. *Things Fall Apart* London: William Heinemann Ltd., 1962.
Aluko, T. M.	*One Man, One Matchet* London: Heinemann Ed. Books, 1968.
Armah, Ayi Kwei	*The Beautyful Ones Are not yet Born* New York: Collier Books, 1969. *Fragments* New York: Collier Books, 1971. *Why Are We So Blest?* London: Heinemann Ed. Books, 1974.
Conton, William	*The African* London: Heinemann Ed. Books, 1966.
Echewa, T. Obinkaram	*The Land's Lord* London: Heinemann Ed. Books, 1976.
Ike, Vincent Chukwuemeka	*The Naked Gods* London: Harvill Press, 1970. *The Potter's Wheel* London: Harvill Press, 1973.
Munonye, John	*Obi* London: Heinemann Ed. Books, 1969. *The Only Son* London: Heinemann Ed. Books, 1969. *A Wreath for the Maidens* London: Heinemann Ed. Books, 1973.
Nzekwu, Onuora	*Blade Among the Boys* London: Hutchinson & Co., 1962. *Wand of Noble Wood* New York: Signet Books, 1961.
Okara, Gabriel	*The Voice* London: André Deutsch Ltd., 1964.
Omotoso, Kole	*The Edifice* London: Heinemann Ed. Books, 1971.

Peters, Lenrie — *The Second Round* London: Heinemann Ed. Books, 1965.
Soyinka, Wole — *The Interpreters* NewYork: Collier Books, 1970.
Season of Anomy New York: The Third Press, 1974.

FRANCOPHONE AFRICAN

Bebey, Francis — *Le fils d'Agatha Mondio* Yaoundé: Editions CLE, 1967.
La poupée ashanti Yaoundé: Editions CLE, 1973.
Béti, Mongo — *Mission terminée* Paris: Editions Buchet/Chastel–Corrêa, 1957.
Perpétue Paris: Editions Buchet/Chastel, 1974.
The Poor Christ of Bomba, trans. Gerald Moore. London: Heinemann, 1971.
Remember Ruben Paris Editions 10/18, 1974.
Le roi miraculé Paris: Buchet/Chastel–Corrêa, 1958.
Dadié, Bernard — *Climbié* Paris: Editions Seghers, 1956.
Diakité, Yoro — *Une main amie* Bamako: Editions Populaires, 1969.
Fall, Malick — *La plaie* Paris: Albin Michel, 1967.
Fantouré, Alioum — *Le cercle des tropiques* Paris: Editions Présence Africaine, 1972.
Kane, Cheikh Hamidou — *L'aventure ambiguë* Paris: Julliard, 1961.
Kourouma, Ahmadou — *Les soleils des indépendances* Paris: Editions du Seuil, 1970.
Laye, Camara — *Dramouss* Paris: Librairie Plon, 1966.
L'enfant noir Paris: Librairie Plon, 1953.
Le regard du roi Paris: Librairie Plon, 1954.
Ouologuem, Yambo — *Le devoir de violence* Paris: Editions du Seuil, 1968.
Oyono, Ferdinand — *Chemin d'Europe* Paris: Julliard, 1960.
Une vie de boy Paris: Presses Pocket, 1970.

Sassine, Williams	*Le vieux nègre et la médaille* Paris: Julliard, 1956. *Saint Monsieur Baly* Paris: Présence Africaine, 1973.
Sembene, Ousmane	*L'harmattan. Livre I: Référendum* Paris: Présence Africaine, 1964. *Les bouts de bois de Dieu* Paris: Presses Pocket, 1971.

Index

Achebe, Chinua, 124–32, 135, 146, 176
African, The, 149–54
Aluko, Timothy Mofolorunso, 132–6, 146, 176
Ambiguous Adventure, 155–60
ambivalence in African view of Europeans
    in Jahoda study, 114–15
    in novels, 118–19, 124, 141
    in oral literature, 97, 99, 101, 103, 109, 111
Angola, 104
Angoulvant, Governor-General Gabriel, 51
Arrow of God, 124–32
Ashanti tribe, 66, 104, 109–11
Azan, Général Paul, 30

Banda tribe, 52–9
Bandi tribe, 108
Batouala, 51–9
Binger, Louis-Gustave, 25–7
Boas, Franz, 8, 24
Bouche, L'Abbé, 25–7
Brazzaville Conference, 29
Broca, Paul, 5

Cameroun, 105
Carus, Carl Gustav, 20
Cary, Joyce, 14, 16, 72, 78–87, 129, 165, 176
Central African Republic, 40, 51–2
Chamberlain, Joseph, 12
characters, African, who contradict stereotypes
    in *The Leopard Priestess*
        Amalagane, 67–9, 71
        Opoku, 67–71
    in *Toum*
        Dela, 73–4

Toum, 74–5
see also intrusions, authorial, to contradict stereotypes
characters, African, who preserve stereotypes
    in *A Yellow Napoleon*
        Feribo, 43–4
        Makindi, 43–4
        Nadu, 43–5
        Tulasi, 41–5
    in *Batouala*
        Bandas, 52–3, 57–9
        Batouala, 52–60
        Bissibi'ngui, 55–6
        Yassigui'ndja, 52–7
    in *Koffi*, Koffi, 59–64
    in *Roman d'un spahi*
        Cora, 32
        Fatou-gaye, 31
        Nyaor-fall, 31, 34
    in *The Heart of the Matter*, Ali, 46–51
characters, African, who transcend stereotypes
    in *A Yellow Napoleon*
        Nadu, 45
    in *Mister Johnson*
        Ajali, 84–5
        Bamu, 87
        Benjamin, 83, 85–6
        Johnson, 78–87, 92, 176
    in *The Land's Lord*
        Ahamba, 165–7
        Philip, 164–5
    in *Va-t'en avec les tiens!*, Doéllé, 88–92
characters, European, who contradict stereotypes
    in *Ambiguous Adventure*
        Lacroix, Jean, 156–7
        Lacroix, Paul, 155–6
        Martial, Lucienne, 157–8

Martial, Pastor, 158-60
  in *Climbié*
    Targe, 145-6
  in *The African*
    Charlie, 149-50
    Hals, Greta, 150-1
    Joe, 149-50
    Morris, Mr. and Mrs., 150
  see also intrusions, authorial, to contradict stereotypes
  see also paired characters
characters, European, who preserve stereotypes
  in *Arrow of God*
    Clarke, 124, 126-9
    Ibo perceptions of Europeans, 131-2
    Winterbottom, 124-7
    Wright, 124, 129-31
  in *Climbié*
    'Gongohi,' 141-3
    judge, the twenty-year old, 143
  in *Houseboy*
    Gilbert, Père, 138-40
    Gosier d'Oiseau, 137-8
    Janopoulos, 136
    Le Commandant, 137
    Madame le Commandant, 140-1
    Moreau, 138-40
    Salvain, 136
    Vandermayer, Père, 139-40
  in *One Man, One Matchet*
    Gregory, Henry, 135-6
    Stanfield, Jim, 132-6
  in *Roman d'un spahi*
    Jean Peyral, 31-4
  in *The African*
    American colonials, 154
    Friedrik, 151
    Schwartz, Miss, and Miss Costello, 154
characters, European, who transcend stereotypes
  in *Mister Johnson*, Rudbeck, 82-3, 165
  in *The Land's Lord*, Father Higler, 161-7, 174
  in *The Radiance of the King*, Clarence, 168-74, 177

  in *Toum*, Monsieur, 72
Climbié, 141-7
Colonial Development Act of 1945, 14
colonialism
  association, policy of, 28
  assimilation, policy of, 12, 21-2, 25-8, 34, 51, 58, 118
  class mobility of colonialists, 15
  'Club', the, 14, 125
  considered permanent or temporary, 28-9
  criticised, 52, 58-9, 76-7, 115-16, 119, 124-32, 134, 141
  endorsed by racist theory, 5, 16
  indirect rule, policy of, 12-14, 28, 119, 124
  prestige of colonialists at home, 15
  segregation in colonies, 14, 28, 33
  supported, 11, 64
Conton, William, 149-54

Dadié, Bernard, 141-7, 176
Dahomey, 25-6, 75
Darwin, Charles
  advocates cranium measurement, 8
  'bestial savage' stereotype in *The Descent of Man*, 5-6
  influence on French colonisers, 30
  polygenesis, effect of Darwinian theory on, 4
  Stanley and Kingsley find 'missing link', 10-11
Delafosse, Maurice, 28
Delavignette, Robert, 28-9, 66, 71-7
Dowd, Jerome, 8

Echewa, T. Obinkaram, 161-7, 174
Ekoi tribe, 103, 105
évolué and *assimilé*
  Dadié as *assimilé*, 147
  Doéllé, 88, 90-1
  Koffi, 59-64
  mask for a French author, 35
  ridiculed in novels, 34
  ridiculed in oral literature, 107-9
  ridiculed in the colonial situation, 118
  stock character, 33

Index

Faivre, Louis *See* Robert Delavignette
Fang tribe, 98
Finot, Jean, 24
Flaubert, Gustave, 51
Fouillée, Alfred, 21
Fralon, Jean, 88
French Equatorial Africa, 52
Fulani tribe, 43
Fulbe women, 33-4

Gambia, The, 149
Garnier, Christine, 78, 87-92
Ghana, 66, 100, 114, 119
Ghezo, King, 26
Gide, André, 52
Gobineau, Count Arthur de, 3, 20-2, 26
Greene, Graham, 16, 40, 46-51, 64, 176
Gueye, Loi Lamine, 28
Guinea, 167

Haggard, Ryder, 15
Hausa tribe, 112-13
Heart of the Matter, The, 46-51
Houseboy, 136-41
Hume, David, 4

Ibo tribe, 124-32, 146, 161, 165
independence movement, 15, 29-30, 38 n.59, 124
Indigénat, 28
intrusions, authorial, to contradict stereotypes
  contrasting technique in Delavignette, 73, 77
  contrasting technique in Kane, 160
  general discussions, 66, 176
  in Conton, 151-4
  in Rattray, 70-1
Ivory Coast, 26, 40, 51, 59, 100, 141

Jabo tribe, 113
Jahoda, Gustav, 114, 119
Johnston, Sir Harry Hamilton, 13
Joseph, Gaston Adrien, ix, 59-64, 90, 176

Kafka, Franz, 168-9, 174 n.4, 5
Kaguru tribe, 98-9

Kane, Cheikh Hamidou, 155-60
Kingsley, Mary, 9, 11
Kipling, Rudyard, 12, 15, 18 n.41, 30
Knox, Robert, 3-5, 20
Koffi, 59-64

Lake District, 149
Land's Lord, The, 161-7
L'aventure ambiguë, 155-60
Laye, Camara, 167-74, 177
Le regard du roi, 167-74
LeBon, Gustave, 21-2
Leopard Priestess, The, 66-71
Letourneau, Charles, 22
Lévy-Bruhl, Lucien, 23
Liberia, 46, 108, 113
Limba tribe, 102, 113
Livingstone, Charles, 9
Livingstone, David, 9
Loi Lamine Gueye, 28
Long, Edward, 5
Loti, Pierre, 30-5, 59, 75
Louis XV, 27
Lugard, Lord, 13, 15, 28, 126

Mangbetu tribe, 97
Maran, René, 40, 51-9, 63-4
Maunier, René, 29
miscegenation, 21, 43
Mister Johnson, 78-88
monogenesis, 4, 20, 25
Morton, Samuel George, 8, 20
Mphahlele, Ezekiel, 154
mulattoes, half-castes, 4, 9-10, 15, 32, 41-5

Negritude, 51
Neyo tribe, 100
Ngugi, James, 133, 147 n.9
Nietzche, Friedrich Wilhelm, 30
Niger, 71
Niger River, 26
Nigeria
  as setting for novels
    Arrow of God, 124-32
    Land's Lord, The, 161-7
    Mister Johnson, 78-87
    One Man, One Matchet, 132-6
    Yellow Napoleon, A, 40

indirect rule first applied in, 13
  oral literature from, 103, 105, 111
Nkosi, Lewis, 129
'noble savage', 6, 43, 45

One Man, One Matchet, 132–6
oral literature, African, dealing with stereotypes, 97–115
Oyono, Ferdinand, ix, 136–41, 146, 176

paired characters
  'B . . .' and 'Gongohi' in *Climbié*, 141
  'bad' and 'good' characters in *Climbié*, 144
  Clarke and Winterbottom in *Arrow of God*, 127
  general discussion, 118
  Greta and Friedrik in *The African*, 151
  Père Gilbert and Père Vandermayer in *Houseboy*, 139
  Stanfield and Gregory in *One Man, One Matchet*, 133–6
press, role, in popularising stereotypes, 25–6, 37–8 n.35–6
Prix Goncourt, 51
pygmies, 10, 30

Quatre Communes, 28

racism, pseudo-scientific
  Biblical rationale, 4
  central premise, 3
  cranium, measurement of, 8, 27
  hierarchical arrangement of races, 4–5, 11, 20–1
  opponents of, 8, 24
  polygenesis, 4–5, 20
  progeny from interbreeding, 4–5
  stagnation of Negro civilisation, 5, 9
  travellers, confirmed by, 9
  see also related theorists: Broca, Carus, Fouillée, Gobineau, Hume, Knox, LeBon, Letourneau, Lévy-Bruhl, Long, Morton, Tylor
Radiance of the King, The, 167–74
Rattray, Robert S., 66–71, 109–11

Roman d'un spahi, 30–5, 59, 75

Sarraut, Albert, 28
Saussure, Léopold de, 27
Senegal, 28, 30, 155, 167
Senghor, Léopold, 51
Sierra Leone, 40, 46, 102, 113, 149
Southon, Arthur E., 40–6, 64, 176
Spencer, Herbert, 6–7
Stanley, Henry M., 9–10, 30
stereotypes, African, of Americans, Irish, Scots, 119, 154
stereotypes, African, of Europeans
  aloof, 28, 107, 112–14, 116–18, 125, 149
  arrogant, authoritarian, 28–9, 113–16, 118, 127–9, 132, 135, 137, 140–1, 149, 152–4, 172–3
  bored female, 117, 140
  bossy female, 117, 140
  deceitful, 56, 101–4, 112
  disrespectful of Africans, 29, 114, 128, 135, 143
  drunkards, 104, 111, 114
  fluent in local language, 114, 116
  frigid female, 118, 154
  honest, punctual, 114–15
  hypocritical, 104, 139, 154
  immoral, 114–15, 117
  impatient, easily angered, 106, 116, 127–31, 135, 141
  intelligent, 43, 99, 101, 113–14, 116
  lazy, 103, 114
  literate, 98–100, 103, 113, 119, 131–2, 152–3
  materialistic, rich, 56, 97–8, 105–7, 110–15, 131–2
  nymphomaniacal female, 117–18
  paternal, 116, 127–8, 133–4, 139
  racist, cruel, 53–4, 56, 116, 119, 130, 136–9, 143–4, 150
  unable to speak local language, ignorant of local mores, 107, 110, 112, 116, 125
  unclean, 115
  weak in strength and virility, 114
  see stereotype chart, 120–1
  see also ambivalence in African view of Europeans

stereotypes (*Contd.*)
  see also Jahoda, Gustav
  see also oral literature
stereotypes, European, of Africans
  cannabilistic, 10, 16, 26, 30, 57
  childish, 7, 9–11, 16, 21–2, 26–7, 30, 34, 45, 62–3, 114, 117, 137
  cowardly, 21, 26
  deceitful, thieving, 32, 78, 80–1, 84–6, 127
  deficient, mentally, 4–5, 8, 11, 20–2, 25–7, 29, 34, 45, 51, 63, 69, 71, 74, 114
  disrespectful of black women because of polygamy, 6, 32, 54
  drudges (said of black women), 33, 69, 87
  evil, cruel, 6, 8, 10, 15–16, 21, 26, 32, 53–5, 127
  happy-go-lucky, 23, 25–6
  hardy, physically, 5
  infanticide, practise, 6
  lazy, 8, 10, 14, 21, 26, 30, 57, 63–4, 70–1, 76–7, 130, 153
  loyal as servants or soldiers, 15, 21, 26–7, 32, 34, 46–51, 61–2, 78, 81, 130, 164
  monkey-like, 10, 21, 30–2, 114
  musical, good dancers, 10, 13, 21, 30, 32, 34, 130
  oversexed, 8, 21, 23, 25, 32, 45, 53–5, 57–8
  reversion to savagery, 11, 15, 22, 27, 30, 34–5, 42, 59–64, 78–9. See also evolué
  sacrifice, practise human, 16, 25, 41
  savage, 6, 10–11, 15, 26, 63, 91, 125–6
  sex object (said of black women), 32–3, 56–7, 69, 72, 74–5, 88, 131
  superstitious and heathen, 6, 8, 10, 34, 163
  ugly, 10
  unable to display emotion, 7, 23
  undependable, 29, 112
  unstable emotionally, 7, 13, 21, 25, 29, 42, 45, 54
  see also stereotype charts, 35–6

technology, Western
  admiration for in Maunier study, 115
  admiration for in oral tales, 113
  as 'evidence' for racial superiority, 11
  explanatory oral tales for origin of, 99, 101, 115
  Koffi's admiration of, 60
Togo, 87, 91
Toum, 71–7
travellers and explorers, role in popularising stereotypes, 8–12
  see also Binger, Kingsley, Livingstone, Stanley
Twi tribe, 100, 110
Tylor, Edward, 8

Ubangi-Shari, see Central African Republic
Upper Volta, 71

Va-t'en avec les tiens!, 87–92

Une vie de boy, 136–41

'white man's burden' or '*mission civilisatrice*,' 12, 27, 59, 87, 101

Yellow Napoleon, A, 40–6
Yoruba tribe, 111–12, 132

Zola, Emile, 30, 51